To Innovate or Not to Innovate?

A Blueprint for the Law Firm of the Future

Darryl Cooke

Globe Law
and Business

Author
Darryl Cooke

Managing director
Sian O'Neill

To Innovate or Not to Innovate? A Blueprint for the Law Firm of the Future
is published by

Globe Law and Business Ltd
3 Mylor Close
Horsell
Woking
Surrey GU21 4DD
United Kingdom
Tel: +44 20 3745 4770
www.globelawandbusiness.com

Printed and bound by CPI Group (UK) Ltd, Croydon CR0 4YY, United Kingdom

To Innovate or Not to Innovate? A Blueprint for the Law Firm of the Future

ISBN 9781787422483
EPUB ISBN 9781787422490
Adobe PDF ISBN 9781787422506
Mobi ISBN 9781787422513

DISCLAIMER
This publication is intended as a general guide only. The information and opinions which it contains are not intended to be a comprehensive study, or to provide legal advice, and should not be treated as a substitute for legal advice concerning particular situations. Legal advice should always be sought before taking any action based on the information provided. The publishers bear no responsibility for any errors or omissions contained herein.

To my wonderful mother who has given so much,
and my two terrific boys, Ashley and Hayden,
who have so much to give.

Endorsements

"Whereas entrepreneurs break rules, the discipline of law tends to be ruled by precedent, resulting in a cultural lack of innovation. Lawyers cannot be trusted advisers in name only, for it involves an ongoing change process founded on innovated service, care and, above all, value in relationships, communication and negotiation. Learning to adapt so that innovation is the norm is simple to say yet hard to achieve and such guides for lawyers are few. That's why it was so refreshing to read Darryl Cooke's book, *To Innovate or Not to Innovate*. Its accessible style highlights the innate challenges to overcome and introduces the right solutions for a law firm to shed century-old thinking, question routines and make a real difference, whilst maintaining the very best of its profession's heritage."

Colin Turner, CEO mentor, entrepreneur and author of *A Brave New Business World*

"This is a book designed for leaders who wish learn how to inject an effective dose of innovation into their organisations. It is an easy read and the ideas in it are absolutely sound. If well applied, they could work for any type or size of organisation."

Chris Daffy, service strategy specialist, consultant and author

"Creating a really innovative change programme in a traditional industry such as the law is clearly a big and demanding subject. There can be no magic bullet to achieve it, but Darryl Cooke's book adds real value by bringing out a practical roadmap and specific initiatives that firms can implement to make real progress in what seems a daunting but necessary task."

Simon Inchley, private equity investor and serial entrepreneur

"Darryl Cooke has woven together his considerable management knowledge with his success and experience in law firm management to answer the anguished cries of 'decent people forced to work long hours at a job they don't like, under conditions they cannot control, for clients who do not express appreciation'. Cooke rightly concludes that the management of law firms is 'an awesome responsibility' because management decisions don't just impact those who work at the firm – those decisions also impact their families and friends. Sprinkled throughout the stories, discussions and facts supporting why and how firms can evolve are many insightful (and for law firms, revolutionary) Cooke-isms. Managing partners who are truly concerned about the lives of those working at the firm and who wish to create an enduring legacy should take serious note of the ideas expressed in this book."

Mitchell Kowalski, strategic adviser on legal operations and author of *The Great Legal Reformation and Avoiding Extinction: Reimagining Legal Services for the 21st Century*

Table of contents

Introduction

As long as you live, keep learning how to live.
Seneca

Lawyers are not known as creative people. If they had wanted to be creative, they would have become architects or interior designers or city planners. In general, being able to understand regulations or case law does not require an enormous amount of creativity. Assimilating vast amounts of information and applying knowledge to the interpretation of regulations does not necessarily require a creative mind. At the same time, the leadership in a law firm rarely looks beyond its own people for inspiration. A managing partner usually begins his or her rise to the top from within the organisation, beginning as a trainee. On a Friday evening he or she may be a tax or corporate lawyer or litigator and by Monday morning he or she may be managing a £100 million business with no business or leadership credentials whatsoever. The knowledge to bring about change and breathe innovation into the organisation simply does not exist. And neither is there deemed to be the need. The law has long been one of the most profitable industries there is. Why change? Ever since the *American Lawyer* started to introduce the measure of profits per partner in the United States, closely followed by the United Kingdom, the only thing a managing partner is interested in to guarantee his or her longevity is increasing the profits of the equity partners. That way, the best lawyers are retained and the firm attracts the best in the market. To achieve that, all he or she has to do is squeeze more chargeable hours out of the firm's lawyers – in particular its junior lawyers. Whereas 1,300 or so hours *per annum* was once the norm, young lawyers are now expected in many firms to do 2,000 hours or more. A term has emerged in London to describe this new form of voluntary slavery – 'beasting'. The model therefore is simple – recruit the lawyers, set them an uncomfortable annual hourly target and charge them out at as high an hourly rate as you possibly can. And as long as we all do the same so that the client has no alternative, we can continue to ensure that our partners become millionaires. And so comes to fruition the worst management maxim of all time – 'if it ain't broke, don't fix it'. The death of innovation. The scourge of creativity. And who loses? In the long run, everyone loses. Certainly the client who does not benefit from an evolving modern legal service with new ideas to aid their business; definitely the young lawyer whose passions and ambitions of joining a glorious profession with a desire to serve are stolen; and eventually the self-serving partner who will see change imposed in ways he or she cannot yet envisage unless he or she can get out in good time with his or her monies well invested.

Michael Hayman and Nick Giles in their excellent book *Mission: How the Best in Business Break Through* (Portfolio Penguin, 2016) describe how businesses make a difference in a fast-changing and innovative world, where commentators report that two-thirds of the companies that will make up the S&P stock market index in a decade's time have yet to be created. We live in a time where Uber has changed the transport industry, Amazon has turned the book and the retail industries upside down, Airbnb has transformed how we holiday and Google ... well, Google helps us to find new ways to understand the world we live in. But why didn't Waterstones or Barnes & Noble launch Amazon, or Thomas Cook launch Airbnb? They had the knowledge, the capacity and the revenues. But when you have a successful model with strong revenues and profits you are less likely to seek to change your model. Real change often comes about when there is real need. Business thought leader John Kotter[1] refers to it as starting with "a sense of real urgency". A time when failing to change would lead to extinction. In essence, when there is no alternative.

This is not a book just about innovation but a book about growth. Every senior and managing partner is seeking new growth. Once the core business of a company has matured, finding that growth can become elusive. How do fast-growing companies such as Amazon, Netflix or Airbnb maintain that growth? How can new growth be generated in a mature industry? Why do leaders in these businesses fail? Do they become risk averse? When they accept that growth is not attainable, they accept that the only way to deliver improved profits per partner is to massage the key figures. Demand more hours from the lawyers, increase the charge out rate, implement a lateral hire programme. That, for a short time, can bring about lower single-digit growth but no more than that. To achieve real growth requires real change. There are only three ways of increasing revenues in a law firm. One is to obtain more transactions or work from existing clients, the second is to charge more for the work and the third is to attract more clients. Innovation and delivering greater value is at the heart of all three. It makes all three easier to achieve.

As with so much else, innovation is a process. Rarely does an idea for a new growth business emanate from the head of an employee. However, if it does, it must be valued, encouraged, shaped and modified until it becomes something real – a business plan and an accompanying action plan. Along the way it will face antagonism and negative voices arguing eloquently (as is a lawyer's way) against it. In such an environment all innovation will be strangled at birth and it is unlikely that further ideas will appear. Why would they?

In order to overcome such negativity and to generate new ideas on a regular basis, a culture of innovation must be created. An infrastructure that supports innovation and lauds innovators as the real heroes in a business must be established. Negative naysayers must be marginalised. Failure must become acceptable.

Creativity in a corporate environment does not just depend on an individual as was the case with Jobs and Wozniak when they assembled the first Apple computer in Jobs's garage. It depends just as much on the infrastructure and environment. Not just physically, but how well suited the environment is to the diffusion of ideas. Jobs and Wozniak had the freedom to go in any direction they wanted. They had a passion and an attitude to change the world. They were not hampered by the politics, the bureaucracy or the resistance to change that is often found in large organisations. At the outset they answered to themselves and to no one else.

Chapter 1

If it ain't broke, don't fix it

If there was nothing wrong in the world, there wouldn't be anything for us to do.

George Bernard Shaw

A longstanding client of my firm describes his R&D department as standing for "rob and duplicate". He says it tongue-in-cheek but he is not far from the truth. Innovation occurs usually as a result of different personal experiences, often subconscious, converging on each other to create a new and better way. David Kord Murray describes in his book *Borrowing Brilliance*,[2] the six steps to business innovation by building on the ideas of others.

In his brilliantly researched book *The Innovators*, Walter Isaacson describes the invention of the computer as an evolution of scientific minds drawing on each other's knowledge over a period of more than 150-years.[3]

This period stretched from Charles Babbage's invention of the Analytical Engine in the early 1800s – a general-purpose computer that could carry out a number of different tasks based on programming instructions given to it and which was formed as a result of combined innovations that had been developed in other fields – to the work undertaken by Alan Turing at Bletchley Park, Howard Aiken, Konrad Zuse, Claude Shannon and George Stibitz at Bell Labs, John Atanasoff, John Mauchly and the US War Department's funding of ENIAC as part of the war effort.

Peter Galison, the Harvard science historian, refers to this evolution as a 'trading zone'. According to Isaacson: "When these disparate practitioners and theoreticians came together, they learned how to find a common parlance to trade ideas and exchange information."[4]

And, of course, innovation does not end at the invention of the computer but continues with the work done by Texas Instruments, Hewlett Packard, Intel, Microsoft, Apple, Tim Berners-Lee, Google and IBM to create the digital revolution that continues apace.

As Isaacson writes in *The Innovators*:

One way to look at innovation is as the accumulation of hundreds of small advances, such as counters and punch card readers. At places like IBM, which specialise in daily improvements made by teams of engineers, this is the preferred way to understand how innovation really happens. Some of the most important technologies of our era, such as the fracking techniques developed over the past six decades for extracting natural gas, came about because of countless small innovations as well as a few breakthrough leaps.[5]

Of course, if companies were to adopt the management maxim 'if it ain't broke, don't fix it' then no progress would be made until there was no other way or, to use Daryl Conner's analogy, as referenced by Kotter in his eight-step change model, a 'burning platform' has occurred. 'If it ain't broke, don't fix it' kills vision, passion, innovation and the excitement of being different.

Innovation is essential to the forward movement of a business. Standing still means that you watch your competitors pass you by. It rarely happens quickly but it will certainly happen if you do not prepare for the future.

Kaizen is the Japanese word for improvement. '*Kai*' means change and '*zen*' for the better. It is a business philosophy. It is about continuous improvement in a business looking at all parts of the business, the product, the people and the process. It is a daily process that goes beyond simple productivity improvement. It becomes a culture of small aligned and focused improvements. It can be all types and all sizes of improvements. The important thing is that it creates a culture of improvement at every level.

Kaizen has been at the heart of many companies' success. When established as a philosophy in a business it is built into every level and becomes part of everything a company does. It has to be adopted by everyone, practised every day and everywhere.

Dr W Edwards Deming, a statistician who went to Japan to help with the census after World War II, taught statistical process control to leaders of prominent Japanese businesses. His message was that by improving quality, companies will decrease expenses as well as increase productivity and market share. He created 14 key principles for management to follow in order to improve the effectiveness of a business or organisation, which can be downloaded from the The W Edwards Deming Institute.[6]

Kaizen has become one of the core principles of the Toyota production system. It is described by Toyota as a quest for continuous improvement. Toyota has adopted the slogan "always a better way".

It is described by Toyota as:

a philosophy that helps to ensure maximum quality, the elimination of waste, and improvements in efficiency, both in terms of equipment and work procedures. Kaizen improvements in standardised work help maximise productivity at every worksite. Standardised work involves following procedures consistently and therefore employees can identify the problems promptly.[7]

Toyota describes the philosophy as humanising and empowering the workplace and it allows individual members to identify areas for improvement and suggest practical solutions. The focused activity surrounding solution finding is often referred to as a *kaizen blitz* where activities are focused around a process or product for a short period of time and solutions sought at all levels.

"Brailsford believed in a concept referred to as the 'aggregation of marginal gains'; that if you improved every area related to cycling by just 1%, then those small gains would add up to a remarkable improvement."

In 2010, Dave Brailsford became the performance director at British Cycling. He led the rise of Team GB Cycling and, ultimately, of the incredible Olympic success in 2012. No British cyclist had ever won the *Tour de France*, but as the new general manager of Team Sky Brailsford was asked to change that. His approach was simple.

Brailsford believed in a concept referred to as the "aggregation of marginal gains"; that if you improved every area related to cycling by just 1%, then those small gains would add up to a remarkable improvement: "Put simply ... how small improvements in a number of different aspects of what we do can have a huge impact to the overall performance of the team."[8]

This means that no stone is left unturned. Everything is measured and analysed, everything is challenged, and improvement is sought at every stage.

They started by optimising the things you might expect: the nutrition of riders, their weekly training programme, the ergonomics of the saddle and the weight of the tyres.

But Brailsford and his team did not stop there. They searched for 1% improvements in tiny areas that were overlooked by almost everyone else: discovering the pillow that offered the best sleep and taking it with them to hotels, testing for the most effective type of massage gel, and teaching riders the best way to wash their hands to avoid infection. They searched for 1% improvements everywhere. During Bradley Wiggins' *Tour de France* win they arranged to have his bed moved to each overnight stop to ensure a good night's sleep.

As Brailsford said when interviewed by the BBC:

The whole principle came from the idea that if you broke down everything you could think of that goes into riding a bike, and then improved it by 1%, you will get a significant increase when you put them all together.

There's fitness and conditioning of course, but there are other things that might seem on the periphery, like sleeping in the right position, having the same pillow when you are away (or even bed) and training in different places ... They're tiny things but if you clump them together it makes a big difference.[9]

Brailsford believed that if they could successfully execute this strategy, then Team Sky would be in a position to win the *Tour de France* within five years. He was wrong – they won it within three years.

In 2012, Team Sky rider, Bradley Wiggins, became the first British cyclist to win the *Tour de France*. That same year, Brailsford coached the British cycling team at the Olympic Games and dominated the competition by winning 70% of the gold medals available. In 2013, Team Sky repeated their feat by winning the *Tour de France* again, this time with rider Chris Froome. Many have followed the approach taken by British Cycling.

Brailsford was right. If you could make 1% improvements in lots of areas then the cumulative effect was immense. He developed a culture at British Cycling of constant improvement – *kaizen*. He looked for problems so that he could improve on them.

By analysing mechanics in the team truck, he discovered that dust was accumulating on the floor and thus undermining bike maintenance, and so he had the floor painted pristine white so that impurities could be detected more easily. Each weakness was a threat but by addressing them they could become an opportunity. While the competition ignored this obsession, Brailsford, by focusing on small changes, could create an advantage. These small advantages not only created real benefits but they also created increased confidence in the minds of the riders.

Whether you call it the aggregation of marginal gains or *kaizen*, gradual improvement has revolutionised sport. But as Matthew Syed in his book *Black Box Thinking* explains, it also has a major role to play in just about any business.[10] In business, many of the most innovative companies are now using a marginal gains approach. Google runs 12,000 data-driven experiments annually in order to discover small weaknesses and so make small improvements. One experiment found that by tweaking the colour of the toolbar from darker to lighter blue it increased the number of click throughs.

The challenge for law firms and professional services practices is how to develop an infrastructure that embraces a culture of change and improvement. The law is often referred to as the oldest profession. Law firms for years have been hemmed in by antiquated regulations. Law firms have mistakenly promoted leaders from within and have not been exposed to the experiences of other industries. Yet, in spite of that, they have remained increasingly profitable and so the need for change has not seemed necessary. They have been told that the world is changing and have seen quiet revolutions in other industries. They have been told that there is a technological revolution coming and that life will never be the same. They have encountered attacks on all sides – from technology, from accountants, from alternative business structures – yet they have maintained their margins and continued to focus on profits per partner as their driver.

John Kotter, the Harvard Business School leadership and change guru, writes about the eight steps of change management which have become the classical approach to change management, and Daryl Conner's analogy of the 'burning platform' has been expounded by many change gurus the world over. This analogy comes from the burning of the oil rig at *Piper Alpha* in Scotland where, in 1988, 166 crew members and two rescuers lost their lives.

One of the injured crew members found himself on the platform edge and faced the decision whether to stay on the platform and hope to be rescued or jump into the water below. He knew that he would not survive for long if he was not rescued and so took the decision to jump from the platform into the water.

When asked why he'd jumped he said: "It was either jump or fry." He jumped quite simply because he felt he had no choice but to do so – the price of staying on the platform was just too great.

Law firms are not yet facing this burning platform. Their 'burning platform' is masked by their ability to increase profits per partner by increased hours from junior lawyers. But Waterstones did not respond to the arrival of Amazon and Walmart did not respond to Amazon's move into general retail, and both have now been outgrown by Amazon. Kodak was in denial when digital photography came along and saw its film-based business disappear within decades. Kodak had a 10-year window of opportunity to prepare for the change and yet despite its vast resources did very little to prepare for it. But the 10-year opportunity window that Kodak enjoyed and wasted is fast eroding in the world of the law firm and the 'burning platform' is becoming ever more likely.

New technologies will certainly play a part but even more than that will be the growth of alternative business structures that can accommodate the superstar lawyers and their demand for rising incomes. New structures that accommodate the top rainmakers and their demands will do irreparable damage to some firms. On top of that, technology will hit firms at the lower end.

Law firms stick to what they know. Innovation in general merely plays an aesthetic role because it is the new fashion. Lawyers are conservative by nature and gaining the support of hundreds of partners to make a significant change is nigh on impossible. And so long as it is possible to work harder and charge more, where is the need?

The advent of behavioural economics provides the catalyst to understanding both the needs of a firm's clients and its people. Practitioners of behavioural economics can be found in most leading universities around the world, as well as in government agencies and increasingly so in major corporations, as they seek to understand how their clients will behave when faced with their products and services.

Economic rationality influenced thinking for many years. Gary Becker and the Chicago School psychologists offered a reality check to prevailing economic thinking. But it was Amos Tversky and Daniel Kahneman who published a number of papers which appeared to undermine the ideas about human nature held by mainstream economics. They are perhaps best known for the development of 'prospect theory', which shows that decisions are not always optimal. Our willingness to take risks is influenced by the way in which choices are framed, that is, it is context-dependent.

Which of the following would you prefer?:
1. *(A) A certain win of £250, versus*
   (B) A 25% chance to win £1,000 and a 75% chance to win nothing?
2. *How about:*
   (C) A certain loss of £750, versus
   (D) A 75% chance to lose £1,000 and a 25% chance to lose nothing?[11]

Tversky and Kahneman's work shows that responses are different if choices are framed as a gain (1) or a loss (2). When faced with the first type of decision, a greater proportion of people will opt for the riskless alternative (A), while for the second problem people are more likely to choose the riskier (D). This happens because we dislike losses more than we like an equivalent gain – giving something up is more painful than the pleasure we derive from receiving it.

Kahneman and Tversky's work was built upon by Ariely in his book *Predictably Irrational* and even more by Richard Thaler in his book *Nudge*.[12] A lot of the early work was built around pricing and value perception and has become invaluable in the way that businesses will often approach the setting of pricing policies. But the work done by Thaler led to a much wider use of the knowledge gained from a study of behavioural economics, from buying an alarm clock or buying football tickets to applying for a mortgage. It soon became recognised by government and the 'nudge' unit was formed at 10 Downing Street. The principle was based on libertarian paternalism. In general, people should be free to do what they wish but they should be encouraged to make the right decisions. Fruit will be put at eye-level but junk food will not be banned. One of the earliest nudge successes was amending legislation so that you had to actively opt out of a workplace pension scheme rather than opt in. That simple nudge moved participation from 60% to over 80%.

Although it is still a recent science, businesses are quite rightly waking up to the power of understanding the often irrational thinking processes of customers when purchasing their products or the unexpected motivations of their employees when joining a business, or that they are often motivated by factors other than money to give their best to an organisation. It is the reason why many large businesses will now employ their own behavioural economists. To be truly innovative it is essential to understand not only the rational behaviour of clients but also their often irrational behaviour.

The law firm model of a myopic focus on profits per partner and setting out to achieve it by financial engineering of its manageables of chargeable hours and hourly rate fails to acknowledge the needs of the client. And, moreover, it offers no incentive to understanding and innovating. Lawyers are often seen as the least commercial of the professional services and it is no wonder why.

Change must come from the very top and be sponsored by the whole leadership team. That is where it starts but to achieve the change in culture that is needed requires the whole firm to be part of that change. Therefore, everyone in the practice must understand the need for innovation and want it, otherwise it will become a six or 12-month fad and no sustainability will have been achieved. As Dale Carnegie said: "Those convinced against their will are of the same opinion still."[13] I was once on the board of a top-10 law firm when values were discussed at a partners' away day. Various values were put up individually on the screen and partners were asked to stand up for any value that they felt the firm should incorporate. Innovation came across the screen and I stood up – sadly, I was the only partner standing. It would be nice to think of that as unusual and not representative of other firms. I know that is not the case.

Innovation cannot be left to consultants or to support staff, or junior partners or associate lawyers. It must be owned by the senior partner and the managing partner. Leadership is everything and the leader must have followers, otherwise, the leader is just going for a disorganised ramble.

Chapter 2
Leadership is everything

A leader is a dealer in hope.

Napoleon Bonaparte

Leadership sets the vision of an organisation and it determines the culture. Creating the change that is needed must come from the very top. The great tendency in law firms is to undertake surveys and ask the opinion of everyone. Seth Godin wrote: "If I listened to feedback, I would have quit on the first day."[14] There is no doubt that listening is an incredibly important part of leadership but so is backing your own experience and intuition. If you have any doubt, read *Blink* by Malcolm Gladwell.[15] Henry Ford is supposed to have said, although it may of course be apocryphal: "if I'd asked the customers we'd have just had faster horses", and Steve Jobs certainly said: "people don't know what they want until you show it to them".[16] But my favourite example of conviction leadership is that given by Martin Luther King Jr who was continually asked by many of his supporters to abandon his non-violent movement in favour of the violent approach promulgated by Malcolm X. In response, he said that he refused to determine what is right by taking a Gallup poll of the trends of the time. To explain his position, he said that there were leaders in Germany who sincerely opposed what Hitler was doing to the Jews. But they took their poll and discovered that anti-Semitism was the prevailing trend, and in order to keep in step with the times they yielded to Hitler. How different history would have been if they had followed their own convictions.

In an age of information overload, Gladwell explains, with example after example, the power of experience and backing your intuition. You are where you are because you have the experience, the training and the knowledge. Back your judgement.

You are the leader because people recognise that you are the best for your position. Yes, they want you to listen, empathise and understand but they also want you to be you, to use your experience and emotional intelligence and not be waylaid by focus groups or surveys. They want you to lead.

Leadership is about envisioning a brave future, about giving direction and exciting the organisation by showing just what is possible. Introducing innovation into a law firm culture is not as easy as it first seems. It is one thing to suggest that the firm should look at different ways of doing things, but it is quite another to change the culture and make innovation a key value of the firm. But it is only by doing that, by changing the values of the firm so that innovation becomes one of the most prized parts of its personality, that innovation will become a real and constant characteristic of the firm. It is only then that innovation will really occur, either as an aggregation of marginal gains or with major leaps forward.

But do not underestimate the need for great leadership.

Two of the best and now classical business books of all time were written by Jim Collins and Jerry Porras.[17] The first, *Built to Last*, was one of the most in-depth studies and analyses of why great companies have become great following a study of 18 of the largest and most visionary companies of the last century. The second, *Good to Great*, was an even more in-depth study of why some companies make the leap to be great and others do not. Collins and Porras used 21 research associates over a five-year period and examined nearly 1,500 Fortune 500 companies. In

Good to Great Collins and Porras develop the idea of five levels of leadership – Level 1 being a highly capable individual who makes effective contributions through talent and good work habits, through to a Level 4 leader who creates higher performance by creating and pursuing a compelling vision, and finally a Level 5 leader who through a blend of personal humility and professional will builds enduring greatness into an organisation.

Collins and Porras write in *Good to Great* that they found Level 5 leaders at the helm of every good to great company during the transition period. They describe them as self-effacing individuals who showed a fierce resolve to do whatever is required in order to make the company great:

Level 5 leaders channel their ego needs away from themselves and into the larger goal of building a great company. It's not that Level 5 leaders have no ego or self-interest. Indeed, they are incredibly ambitious – but their ambition is first and foremost for the institution, not themselves.

Before embarking on change and developing a culture to encourage innovation and change, the leader must consider his or her own leadership and his or her ability to develop followers and to foster support for the change that is forthcoming. He or she is quite likely leading a company whose sole focus is to improve profits per partner. After all, an increase in profits per partner will satisfy all of his or her main stakeholders, it will retain the best partners who are less likely to be enticed away, and it will help to secure better lateral hires. The simplest and easiest way to do that is to increase the hourly charge-out rate and/or the number of hours that one of his or her lawyers is required to do each year. However, that is not sustainable and does not allow for an obsessive focus on innovation which is going to take time, will require an attitudinal shift and does not guarantee the increase in profits required. But when it is done right it can separate the firm from its competition and create pathways to new markets and, ultimately, better profits.

It is up to the leader to create the vision, encourage followers who will also become leaders and put in place new habits that will deliver the vision. To achieve that, it is likely that a leader will have to look again at his or her management system. To put innovation at the heart of the firm the leader will need to address the bureaucracy and put much more control into the hands of others. He or she will need to manage strategies instead of budgets and being slaves to a plan. Can a leader do this? That is, can he or she tear down the bureaucracy and budgets and build an empowered organisation, while at the same time maintaining focus, coordination and control? To do so, a leader needs to introduce a different belief system to the organisation. The leader must move the firm away from a command-and-control system and promote leaders who naturally adopt a style that emphasises values, purpose, humility and service. Before change and before innovation must come a leadership and management framework and infrastructure that will allow innovation to flourish. One difficult manager in an organisation can block and irreparably damage the whole culture of innovation. Optimism is a force multiplier. It comes from the top but must then cascade all the way down the firm and into every nook and cranny. We have all seen the damage that a respected individual can do if they choose not to buy into proposed changes. This challenge cannot be shirked but must be faced up to from the outset. In a professional services organisation the task is made harder because the individuals who can cause the most damage are often partners who are not part of the executive management team, or even the non-executive leadership team, but who may be successful client partners with large client revenues and client loyalty to give them negotiating strength within their firms. It is a brave managing partner that takes such individuals on. Did I mention that bravery is a requisite of a great leader who is prepared to change the culture?

No matter how frustrating it may be, the managing partner and/or the senior partner needs to bring all key people with him or her.

Leading edge, fast-growing and innovative companies are deeply committed to the firm's purpose, its values and its success, and act with a high level of energy and ambition. Their leaders have autonomy and authority to make decisions; they are principled, share information, know what is expected of them and are open and authentic; they are passionate; they have determination to succeed; they are accountable and take full responsibility for the way they work and their performance; they find pleasure in the work they do and with their colleagues; and they share a sense of community and trust. They care. The question is how do they achieve that?

It can only be achieved when the leader leads by example, working closely with his or her immediate team and drawing them together. There needs to be a move from command-and-control to values determined by the team, to processes agreed upon by the team, to a way of working that is agreed by the team so that a level of performance is expected by everyone and there is an agreed transparency and accountability. This can only be achieved when time is spent with a leader who is not defensive but who uses his or her experience and knowledge to enhance, not dominate, the debate. Questions such as those below should be regularly discussed at length and often revisited so everyone knows the framework from which the business operates and which guides the decision making of everyone in the business.

- Why do we exist as a firm?
- What are we passionate about?
- How do we make money?
- Who are our most important clients?
- How would our clients describe our firm?
- What is our brand?
- What would we like our story to be?
- What is our proven process?
- What products/services do our clients value most?
- Are our clients' needs changing?
- What is our value offering?
- Who are our competitors and what threats do they pose?
- What is our 10-year plan/three-year plan/12-month plan?
- What obstacles need to be overcome in order to achieve our plan?
- Which partners are going to struggle with change?

- Which partners can we count on?
- What values are most important to us?
- What behaviours do we expect from everyone in the firm?
- Do we like our firm?
- Do our people enjoy working here? Have we created a family?

These are questions not just for the executive team but also for the non-executive leadership team to address, as well as key performing partners: the key ambassadors in the firm who, if not handled carefully, can cause ripples in the pond.

These are often questions that a client partner will not have faced before and because of his or her singular focus on the clients will not necessarily see the value to the practice. After all, it seems that he or she will have achieved success without it. He or she will have personal values which will be all about delivery to the clients but will see the firm's values as fluffy and not relevant to him or her. Therefore, the leader needs to spend a lot of time framing and helping these partners to understand both the reason for the questions and the need for change in the wider organisation and, most of all, how it will help the partner. Only then can the leader seek personal support from those partners for his or her leadership.

Management systems

It is almost impossible to develop a culture of innovation under a command-and-control management system. Generally, management thinking has moved in this direction over the last few decades and most writing will bear this out. But the best writing I have found that expounds this thinking clearly and comprehensively is that of Hope, Bunce and Röösli in *The Leaders Dilemma: How to Build an Empowered and Adaptive Organization Without Losing Control* (Wiley, 2011). They describe the now out-of-date command-and-control system as "stifling". It inevitably stifles both creativity and the desire to go beyond the expected. In a command-and-control environment, a leader's job is usually to act as a manager for shareholders or stakeholders with the aim of maximising shareholder value and, in the case of a law firm, profits per partner. It is built on a short-term model to deliver enhanced profits each year which is at odds with a long-term focus on innovative approaches to a business. The essence of the model is often that of detailed plans and budgets to enable managers to predict and control future outcomes. It is believed that simply setting out mission and strategy statements will lead to employees giving greater commitment. No thought is given to engagement. Leaders under this system believe that they can control the organisation through detailed rules and regulations and by telling people what to do, irrespective of what they believe or want. They manage risk carefully. Information is restricted and carefully controlled so people only see what they need to see. Honesty is rare and things are portrayed in a good light all the time. The aim of budgets and targets is to create an efficient organisation. Each function is generally encouraged to focus on its own area and budget. It kills the spontaneity (and fun) of working across groups and creating a dynamic, one-purpose organisation. Generally, local managers will have to go up the line before decisions are made, assuming that only those at the top have the experience to deal with matters. This kills both creativity and dynamism. Accountability is a matter of pleasing the boss and not of delivering for the organisation. Goal-setting and the formulation of objectives are put forward as the magic formula for improving motivation, and targets are generally of a financial nature. Leaders in this system of management also believe in personal rewards for targets achieved. The belief is that this is the only way to challenge and motivate people. Strategy is top down and relies on telling people what they have to do and that performance will be measured against the plan. Resources are allocated to meet the plan and, thus, are distributed ineffectively. The system is not only outdated but fails to unleash in a business the hidden ambition and innovation. Innovation must come through the whole organisation as a leader seeks improvement at every level and in every area. To achieve this, a new system of trust and belief should be put in place.

"Leaders promote information flow and introduce new levels of openness and transparency. They believe that if everyone can be trusted to see the same information then they will make the right decisions quickly."

In a system where command-and-control is not exercised but where people are organised around and motivated by a vision that everyone buys into, leaders do not accept that shareholder interests are paramount. Leaders accept that all stakeholders including employees, clients, suppliers, communities and partners need to have a healthy balance. Leaders in this system treat people like the grown-ups they are. The leader needs to communicate a strong vision and invoke pride and passion (as well as peer pressure) to achieve it. These organisations are aware of risks and processes but operate within a culture of truth, transparency and trust with strong principles. Everyone learns to put the organisation first. They also rely on the exercise of sound judgement throughout the organisation. Leaders promote information flow and introduce new levels of openness and transparency. They believe that if everyone can be trusted to see the same information then they will make the right decisions quickly. People come before profit but, amazingly, by focusing on behaviours the revenues look after themselves. They use processes and systems but the attitude around them is different. They do not become mere box-tickers but have real value and judgement. The purpose of the system is never forgotten, and that is to produce a higher quality service. Leaders believe that in order for his or her employees to be accountable for their performance they need freedom and authority to make decisions. By empowering the decision making they will create more imaginative and innovative people. They are not part of the problem but part of the solution. The purpose of senior executives is to set high standards, to set the goals and ambitions and to create a pathway to allow their teams to achieve them and always to act as guides, mentors and coaches. The aim of senior executives should be to continue to set the goal high. A goal set too low leads to little change. Stretching the goals will mean that everything has to be considered and new ideas start to flow. Leaders in this system understand the power of recognition and build reward-based systems around that, while also developing a culture where failure is just part of the journey. There is no such thing as failure. The only failure is not trying. There are no bad soldiers, only bad officers.

Mitchel Resnick of MIT compares this type of management system to that of a flock of birds. Most bird flocks do not have leaders at all. But each bird follows a set of rules, for example, aligning themselves in flight to create maximum velocity, taking turns at leading and dropping back to help sick or struggling birds. As a result, the organisation operates as an integrated system.

Trust and serve

I call this system of leadership 'trust and serve'. The leader sets the vision and communicates it simply and clearly and continues to do that at every opportunity. He or she then trusts his team while seeking to serve their needs and that of the business. Leadership pioneer Ken Blanchard refers to this system as 'servant leadership'.

The most important person in this process is the leader of the business. In a law firm that may be the senior partner or the managing partner. It is likely that one will lead on the initial vision but they must quickly come together as one and support each other at every step. In addition, this is likely to be a major learning curve for the leader particularly if he or she has come through the ranks of the firm. Discipline is key and should include expanding his or her knowledge by reading, attending courses, etc. The one thing that a leader should not do is outsource this process to consultants. He or she can use consultants as a learning wall but must own and deliver the process. Partly because it has to continue after consultants have left, but most of all because he or she needs the respect of the whole business and has to be seen to own and understand the whole project. It will move quickly from a project to a way of life. He or she has to stand up and communicate the ambition and vision of what the firm is setting out to achieve. He or she has to believe in it and to be passionate about it. That is much easier when you become the expert and the fountain of knowledge. At the end of this book I have included a list of suggested books and articles that will give a leader the knowledge he or she needs without the need for consultants. I have seen many firms bring in consultants to lead projects in law firms and I have seen managing partners then accept everything they do with little challenge. This happens because a law firm leader does not feel comfortable operating in a business environment and prefers to hide his or her naivety by defaulting to consultants. That is not good enough and will not work. A leader must do everything to equip himself or herself with the necessary knowledge needed, and not hide behind outside advisers who are not part of the fabric or culture of a business.

John's story

John closes the door gently behind him. His wife is still in bed. The time is 7:00am and this has been the routine for as long as he can remember.

He presses the ignition on the Jaguar F Type, listens to the gentle purr before turning on the DAB radio to listen to Newsday on the World Service. He has done this same journey every weekday, and sometimes weekends, since the day he became equity partner and had been given a car parking space under the building. Some 12 years. And the only thing of comfort has been the sound of the BBC voices on the World Service morning programme. Equity was not the golden glory that John had hoped it would be when he went into the law. John had, like many lawyers, become a lawyer in the idealistic hope of changing the world for the better. An overflow of television dramas and early left-wing tendencies had fuelled this vision of a future where he would change the lives of those less fortunate. Taking articles, now known as a training contract, at a City law firm, because the money was good had very abruptly put an end to this vision which receded quicker than Usain Bolt could run the 100 metres. He now counted himself among the less fortunate. While his friends had built fulfilling and enjoyable lives he had become a slave to the firm. He had wanted to read history – perhaps write a history book – and, even closer to his heart, he had wanted to give his time to a number of charitable causes. But he had become a slave to the chargeable hour and rather than be able to design his life as he had expected when he attained equity, in fact the firm continued to design his life for him. And now time was beginning to run out. He was 52.

But a few weeks ago John had been voted in as managing partner. He had been on the board for a number of years, very likely as a result of his large client billings which had got him the votes he needed, and very likely it was those billings that had got him the role of managing partner, although he had set out a sort of manifesto. John was excited for the first time in a number of years. He was excited about making a difference, about change, about creating a legacy. He knew that to bring about real change he had to bring everyone in the firm with him. He just was not sure that he could do that. But first of all he had to convince his senior partner, a dour, rather boring, conservative and reliable lawyer who was the longest-serving equity partner.

John parked the car in his designated spot next to that of the senior partner. He picked up a café macchiato and was at his desk exactly 75 minutes after leaving the house. An average drive. In precisely 45 minutes time he was to meet with his senior partner to begin the process of change. If this meeting did not go as planned his dreams would come to an end before they had begun and his time as managing partner would become as frustrating as his time as a board member. It is with this in mind that for the past few months he had devoured business book after business book, self-improvement book after self-improvement book and the occasional book by the new wave of economic behaviourists. Some ideas from these books came flooding back to his mind: become comfortable with the uncomfortable; those convinced against their will are of the same opinion still; and a genuine leader is not a searcher for consensus but a moulder of consensus.

Chapter 3
Building a competitive advantage

It's nice to have valid competition, it pushes you to do better.

Gianni Versace

The heart of strategy is about building a competitive advantage. It is about creating a platform, forming an infrastructure, designing an organisation and from that instilling a belief in your people – all your people – that what you are doing or what you are capable of doing is greater than what can be achieved by your competitors. Your people are your greatest competitive advantage. Leading them is what matters. Without them you are just going for a lonely walk. It is no less and no more than that. It is about overtaking your competitors or about putting blue sky between you and them. At its simplest it is easy: increase revenues, work harder and control costs. But at its most challenging, its most successful and its most game-changing it is about innovation. It is about new and better ways of doing the same things or new ways of doing new things to create better products, provide better services and improve marginal gains. It is also about new ideas – some large and some small. No strategy can be successful without innovation at its core. Businesses do not stand still. If you do stand still, your competitors will pass you by.

Working harder is unsustainable. How many hours can a lawyer work in a year? It is unimaginative and even immoral to drive lawyers to do more and more hours each year. The damage it has on the lawyer coupled with the damage on his or her family should be enough for a leader to rethink his or her business model. At the same time, focusing on pricing sends you racing to the bottom. Price is not everything and when you compete only on price you are accepting commodity status. Play the price game and you are throwing margins to the wind. Not only that but it becomes your primary and often only focus. It kills innovation and it kills value delivery and value innovation. You are accepting that all the client wants is the lowest possible price. Every year buyers of large volumes of legal services will call in their suppliers with the sole aim of reducing prices. The argument will often be that you will make it up on volume. But to enter into this game is a nightmare scenario. You are not Poundland. Price is important to the client but there are other ways of delivering price savings and many other ways of delivering value. A culture without innovation at its heart will immediately go to price; it knows no other way. A culture with innovation at its heart will immediately consider ways of improving value by putting the client at the centre and answering the client's questions: "Why do I do business with you?" and "What do you offer that the other guys don't?"

Michael Porter from Harvard Business School has stated that a competitive advantage can come about in two ways – a cost advantage and a differentiation advantage.[18] The first is obvious but will ultimately damage your business while the second is how the vast majority of businesses find their competitive advantages. This can be interpreted as: Where is the additional value that you bring? Many law firms now look to technology to provide this advantage. This is understandable but technology moves at the speed of light and pouring money into technology is like pouring money into a black hole. The mistake that lawyers often make is that adding value has to be a technical addition or of major substance, whereas it can simply be of an emotional nature. Often personal but definitely with a 'wow' factor.

It is important to begin by identifying the competitive advantages

"Every year buyers of large volumes of legal services will call in their suppliers with the sole aim of reducing prices. The argument will often be that you will make it up on volume. But to enter into this game is a nightmare scenario."

that you already have. It is important to remember that these advantages should be objective and seen to be clear advantages in the minds of your clients. This does not include vague statements such as "we deliver a good service" or even "we have 40 offices" if your client only needs to deal with one office. Competitive advantages are clearly identifiable and quantifiable. Moreover, they are not claimed by your competition – or else it is not an advantage. You will no doubt have some competitive advantages already but they may be hidden away. You may not recognise them as such and as sure as eggs is eggs you will not be communicating them. Ask the question: "What are my firm's most critical advantages?" This is a good question to start with and to ask your employees. It will begin to involve them in the process and you may be surprised. Then consider what are your major clients' competitive advantages and how you would respond to clients when they ask: "Why should I buy from you?", "What is your proven process?", "What do you do that others don't?" and "What could you do that others can't?"

It is these competitive advantages that wins new clients and new deals.

John's story

The automatic door of the garage slowly opened as he edged the Jag forward. It was 7:00pm and he was leaving the office. He switched on the radio and tuned to Jazz FM. Mellow jazz was his chosen genre of music. It helped him to relax on his way home. The day had been good. The meeting with his senior partner had gone particularly well. He had never quite seen eye to eye with the senior partner. They had very different outlooks on life. He had always thought him a very vain man and he found it quite tiresome to hear time and again how much his shoes cost or stories about his tailor. But today was a good day. In fact, he was surprised just how supportive he was. Their thinking was complementary and John felt that their mutual enthusiasm helped to create greater momentum. Perhaps they would never be 'best mates' but they certainly had a shared enthusiasm for what they wanted to do and agreed could be done. John had taken along for his senior partner new copies of a few books that he had been reading that had powered his thinking: *The Leader's Dilemma* by Hope, Bunce and Röösli; *Extreme Teams* by Shaw; and the classic business text *Built to Last* by Collins and Porras.[19] John's senior partner agreed to read them and in a very lawyerly way they agreed that they would discuss things they had taken from their reading from time to time. Once they had stopped enthusing over the possibilities, the senior partner suggested the partners who he felt needed to be brought into their thinking at an early stage. John agreed that this was necessary, like ripples in a pond, and they hatched a plan between them of the best way to do this.

John was very aware that the only way to bring about the growth that he wanted would mean lots of meaningful innovation, not simply what he described as 'aesthetic change', which he believed a lot of his firm's competitors had undertaken. Innovation was the new buzzword. But real innovation meant new and exciting products, perhaps new service areas and probably substantial changes in working practices. That would only be achieved with a change in culture. But John's firm was over 100 years old. And there was no 'burning platform' so convincing partners and staff to change was not going to be easy. Changing a successful business from within is never easy, otherwise Waterstones would have invented Amazon, and Yellow Pages would have invented Google. He knew he had to start with the culture. Innovation had to be at the heart.

A text came up on the car's screen monitor from Vanessa: "Out with Jane and Carly – back about 11 – don't wait up."

John's mind wandered to when he met Vanessa. He had always felt it was the most perfect relationship. They could talk to each other about anything. They seemed the perfect soul mates discussing all things from politics to football to their families and their strange idiosyncrasies, to the inequality that they both felt in the world and what could be done about it. They would talk late into the night. They would talk all the time. Ringing each other up throughout the day just to hear each other's voices and perhaps discuss something in the papers. And they would nearly always agree. They were a real partnership which he thought would be for life. John was not quite sure when things had changed or why they had changed, but they had. Conversation was now in small doses and more often than not they would be passing ships in the night. He did not know what had gone wrong. Had the job taken his soul as well as his time? He tried to think forward to the girls leaving home and what life would be like then, but he couldn't convince himself that they would even be together. The thought saddened him.

He turned into the long drive.

When you look at the competitive advantages that you already have, where do you start? Is that a silly question? With the client of course. Do your services save your client money in ways that your competitor's services do not? Do your services deliver value to your client in ways that your competitors do not? Getting in front of new clients is hard enough. You are more likely to achieve that if you talk their language. We saved this client money so we can do the same for you. Show them how you can save them money or how you can deliver real value. Sometimes you can save them money without you or them realising it. Clients will pay more to get more. That is the reasoning behind added value. But you have to take your services apart and find that added value. Most law firms that I have seen are too lazy to do that. Instead, they focus on the number of offices that they have or number of partners in the firm. Why would the client care? True, it may add to credibility, but if you rely solely on that you underestimate the intelligence of your client. Finding this magic is not easy and most lawyers I know will quickly default to the mundane and workaday, so you have to really challenge and keep momentum going.

And if you do not have any competitive advantages, which is hard to believe, then look at what your competitors are doing or, even better, at other industries and emulate or even improve on them. A study of successful innovators from the past such as Darwin, Newton, Einstein and Edison, and modern innovators like Gates and Jobs shows that each new idea is constructed out of existing ideas. They are all constructed and built on current thinking. So if a client refers to his R&D department as 'rob and duplicate' it is not so wide of the mark, particularly if built in to that is also improvement. Most innovation is the result of evolution over a long period of time and incremental advancements by lots of people. True innovation is a very rare specimen.

In professional services, if you borrow from your competitors you are considered a pirate and unless you can bring significant advancements you are only second to the market; it is very difficult to follow that and become the market leader. But if you borrow from outside your industry, for example, processes from manufacturing, service skills from retail, project management from construction, people skills from sports teams and so on, then you are considered to be a creative genius. This does not mean that you should not look from within the professional services industry but you should not look exclusively from within. We will consider later in the book just how a process to achieve this can be developed.

"Every company has a culture – it will just happen whether you like it or not. The most successful companies design the strategy that their people enjoy being part of and that will lead to the success of the company."

Chapter 4
Culture eats strategy for breakfast

If you want to change the culture, you will have to start by changing the organisation.

Mary Douglas

"Culture eats strategy for breakfast" is a famous quote attributed to Peter Drucker, one of the world's foremost management gurus of the last century. Whether it is just apocryphal or whether it is true, is uncertain. What is not in doubt is the truth of this simple statement. A strong culture can drive a business to success but a good strategy without a compelling culture is unlikely to succeed. It is culture that will turn great strategy into great performance. Every company has a culture – it will just happen whether you like it or not. The most successful companies design the strategy that their people enjoy being part of and that will lead to the success of the company. Netflix is a world leader and ambassador for creating a culture that turned an ordinary company into a very successful company. The Netflix Deck, a document of over 200 slides, is now copied by numerous fast-growing businesses. The culture was begun by chairman and CEO Reed Hastings and developed with his head of HR, Patty McCord. It was not achieved overnight. In fact, it probably took some 10 years but it became a new way of managing people and has become a template for achieving a high-performance culture. The key words in the Netflix Deck are 'freedom' and 'responsibility'. Hastings will often say that he cannot remember when he last made a decision such is the strength of the culture that has now been achieved. Fast-growing companies will almost inevitably have their own culture that defines the business: Airbnb sees its culture as belonging – a feeling of community and connection among employees; Patagonia's culture is that of work hard, play hard – and specifically brings together a group of nature lovers who want to work hard and play hard; and Whole Foods is known for its democratic discipline where giving people a strong voice in how the company is run is paramount while embracing a strong set of performance-enhancing strategies.

Culture in all these cases has been a deliberate choice as to what the company stands for and how it operates day to day.

The Netflix Deck which has been shared and is freely available online is a series of statements that represents what the company stands for. Behind each statement is a clear definition of the statement and what it involves from recruitment to operations.

Culture, like many ideas, has become an overused term and over-developed process. I often feel that is the fault of consultants but that would be incorrect. It is leaders of businesses who abdicate the responsibility of owning culture because they either do not see the importance of it or they do not know how to go about it. It is poor leadership to leave culture in the hands of the HR team. It is the most important asset in your business. If done well it will drive your business forward and will create a momentum that you were not aware was possible. And if you do not know how to do it, then become an expert and do it quickly. There are plenty of books out there and plenty of consultants to advise, and if you cannot find one give me a call. Process to determine culture is important but it has a strong emotional element which the leader must drive. It is the development and growth of an obsession that is shared by every part of the business. It is focusing on a business that everyone would like to be part of and showing every individual in the business how what they do helps in achieving the overall goals of the business but, most of all, it is developing behaviours that make everyone excited about coming into the office because they enjoy a shared obsession with others. To achieve great culture that will drive a business needs great leadership. It begins with vision, it creates an emotional need to desire the vision, and it is achieved by daily specific behaviours and prescribed intentional actions.

Why do teams often succeed over more talented individuals? Why did Barcelona, Bayern Munich or Manchester United dominate their leagues year after year? It is because they had great cultures. Teams where every individual player is prepared to go the extra mile – and the extra mile again – for their team mates. It is easy to win one championship by buying great players and a super-human effort over one season. It is much harder to do it time and time again. That is culture.

When Clive Woodward took over the leadership of the England Rugby Union team he realised that England did not have better players and were unlikely in his lifetime to be better on an individual basis than a southern hemisphere team whose members were better trained and prepared from a young age. The only thing that he could do was to create a better team. When working in industry at Xerox he had read a business book by Paddi Lund, an Australian dentist, called *Building the Happiness Centred Business*.[20] In his book, Lund introduces the concept of courtesy rules. These are very specific rules that are agreed and adopted by a team and that determines their behaviour on a day-to-day basis. They are rules that show each person how to treat another, for example, say 'hello' when you arrive at the office, don't use mobile phones in meetings, brief people properly when handing over a matter, respect someone's holiday time, etc. They take culture and values and they make them specific so that they can work in small teams. The key is that they are determined and agreed by the team. The consequence is that the team members learn to respect each other as they move towards a shared goal. Woodward describes the rules that the England rugby team chose as the glue that joined the team. Interestingly, he never shares the rules. I guess that one of them was 'what happens on tour stays on tour'. But there is little doubt that the England team of 2003 that won the World Cup was a closely knit, determined team whose members would fight to the end for each other. Culture is about values at a macro level; but culture also has to work at a micro level.

To continue the sporting analogies, the New Zealand All Blacks is probably the most successful and enduring sports team ever. To stay the best they have developed a culture that endures no matter who the players are in the team. They have a set of values and they live them. They believe in legacy. They aim to leave the shirt in a better place than they found it. They believe in responsibility. They choose to be leaders not followers. Good leaders create other leaders. It is the responsibility of the CEO to create leaders around him or her. He or she from time to time needs to draw aside from the business, away from the minutiae of the day to day and to look at the needs of the business, and possibly the most important part of that is to create other leaders. Leaders who believe in the culture that the CEO or chairman is trying to develop. They also believe in learning and self-improvement as a critical part of their success. Graham Henry, a former All Black, says "we are always challenging the status quo".[21] It should be no different in business. Tom Peters in *Thriving on Chaos* writes: "Excellent firms don't believe in excellence, only in constant improvement and change."[22] He argues that success is commitment to long-term improvement.

John's story
John pulls out of his driveway. It is 7:00am. The World Service murmurs in the background but he is lost in his thoughts. His mind drifted to why he became a lawyer.

As a young man he was thought to be intelligent (the truth is he just worked harder than his friends). He was a well-educated, sociable, enthusiastic and thoughtful 18 year old. He loved books, Dickens was a particular favourite. He enjoyed music of all genres from classical to indie rock to jazz. He loved film and he was passionate about live theatre. His mother had told him that the world was his oyster. His history teacher had told him that university would open up completely new horizons and had described it as a three-year festival. His A level results were exceptional and he had got a place at a redbrick university to study law. His family was proud. He was excited.

The world was his oyster. He looked forward to listening to recordings of piano concertos and know who was playing. He looked forward to going to classical concerts and knowing when to clap. He wanted to get modern jazz without it all sounding like a terrible mistake and he wanted to know exactly who Procul Harum were (that dates it). He was excited. He wanted to be fully engaged in the world of ideas, to understand economics and just what people see in Bob Dylan. He wanted to possess radical but humane and well-informed political ideals and hold passionate and reasoned debates around wooden kitchen tables saying things like "define your terms" and "your premise is patently specious", and then suddenly discover that the sun has come up and they have been talking all night. He wanted to use words like 'eponymous' and 'utilitarian' with confidence. He wanted to appreciate fine wines, exotic liqueurs and fine single malts – and learn how to drink them without finishing up on a toilet floor – and to eat things like plovers' eggs and lobster thermidor. He wanted to meet new, interesting and exciting people. Most of all he wanted to read – Tolstoy, Dickens, Hardy, Trollope, Murdoch, Fowles. The world really was his oyster. It was all about to come true.

In his first week he signed up to so many clubs that he could hardly carry the literature back with him – sports clubs, golf, soccer, tennis, wine clubs, theatre clubs, film clubs, dining clubs, book clubs. He joined charities. He did not want to be hedonistic but he wanted to give back from all the pleasure he was getting. He loved his life at his university – it was great.

And he was excited about being a lawyer – making a difference and helping people, and being that lawyer that he had seen on the television eating croissants at breakfast meetings and looking very smooth and dapper and handsome. And so he got a place at a major City law firm. Life just could not get better.

During his time at law college he met a wonderful girl, only his second long-term relationship. She was in publishing and at the end of his time at Guildford they moved to London and moved in together. Life was idyllic.

In his first week at his City firm he left the office at 5:00pm. He and his girlfriend Vanessa had tickets for the theatre and for a gig at LSE and also an invite to a university friend's dinner party. They were determined to enjoy London. His mother's words resounded in his head – "the world is your oyster".

The second week, as he was about to leave, he was told to stay to proofread some IPO documents that evening. He rang Vanessa and they postponed their night out with friends. He got home at 11:00pm. The next night he was told that he would be needed at a meeting to go through the verification notes with a client and to process the documents afterwards. He got home at 2:00am. You know the story. It went on and on and on.

They stopped making arrangements to go out because they did not know if he would be home in time. They stopped buying tickets for concerts because there was just no point. He stopped reading and listening to music and going to interesting restaurants. He stopped playing football. He stopped taking an interest in all those things that he was passionate about. He stopped helping a local charity that he had agreed to support. He worked. And he worked. But when the bonuses came around he was rewarded well. It seemed worthwhile – at least for a week or so. But was it?

He became unhappy and even more so when he realised that he was working for other unhappy people. But he was caught – the money was good.

What happens to decent people who are forced to work long hours at a job they do not like, under conditions they cannot control for clients who do not express appreciation or even acknowledge their existence? When people work under these conditions, with little time for personal life and even less time for the outside interests they used to have, they can become bitter, vindictive or passive aggressive. They are not fun to work with; they are not fun to be with.

As he pulled into the office he knew that he had once been a brilliant, entertaining, full-of-life and hungry-to-learn lawyer and human being, and that years of chargeable hours and unreasonable demands by his firm and by clients had made him boring.

John realised that he knew a hundred such lawyers like him and as he switched off the engine he was determined to initiate a change that would alter the lives of those around him – for the better. Today he was going to get the support of a group of people that would be key to this change. It was not going to be easy. He knew they would see him as idealistic. What was that George Bernard Shaw quote? Something along the lines of "some men see things as they are and say 'why?'; I dream of things that never were and say 'why not?'"

You will know when you have got your culture right when you are inundated with job applications for any position in the firm from general office assistant to partner. Until that point you have work to do. And once you understand and have embedded your culture into the organisation, reinforcing your culture begins with your recruitment process. Hiring on values and attitude is critical to the future success. Everyone in the firm must fit. Of course, that also means that along the way you will have to part company with a number of people who do not fit your culture, who become terrorists in the organisation and who will do everything to sabotage it. These people are likely to be in key positions or to be senior and exercise great influence. At the outset you will do everything you can to win them over or at least to negate their negative influence. Optimism is a force multiplier but so, unfortunately, is negativity. You can only allow yourself a limited time to do this otherwise your whole project will be brought down. So, identifying these people at the outset and giving as much time to them as you can early on is very important. Quite often, difficult people just want to be loved and to feel that they are respected. They may surprise you and become your biggest supporters. But if that is not the case then you have to deal with them very swiftly in order that they do not destabilise your plans. That is never easy in a law firm where equity partners in particular are given or assume extraordinary rights that they only see from a personal point of view and not from the firm's point of view. That also is indicative of your culture. Very few partnerships develop a culture with a shared obsession which is what you are trying to achieve. To achieve it you are likely to have to deal with the most selfish of those partners who will always put themselves before the firm. Asking these partners can be difficult but not as hard as some firms make it. The fact is that no one wants to be in a firm where they are not wanted or appreciated. Parting company should be done with decency and courtesy. How you do this will be viewed by everyone in the firm and reflects on your culture.

John's story

John was lost in his train of thought. He had spent the morning with various of his senior equity partners whom he knew that he could call on to give him support. That had gone well. But the afternoon had not gone well when he spent time individually with those partners whom he and his senior partner believed would be difficult. The 'mavericks' as his senior partner called them. The meetings were challenging to say the least. They did not see the need for change. They were worried how it would affect them. They did not think innovation was for lawyers and they certainly thought culture and values were all very well if you worked at Disney but not in a top law firm. Culture meant an easy life to them. They could not afford that with their demanding clients. John explained to them just how important each of them were to the success of the project. He wanted them to be ambassadors and supporters. He wanted each of them to use their massive influence in the firm to act as guides, mentors and leaders to take the firm forward to a new way of thinking and he was prepared to do whatever it took to engage them as leaders in the business. But he had also made it very clear that the firm came first and that if they could not support the project then, as agreed with the senior partner, he would not hesitate to make tough decisions. He had decided that an iron fist/velvet glove approach was always going to provide the most successful result. Talking in the corridors, even silence and not engaging, he explained, would be seen as treachery.

As he headed for home he thought about each meeting in detail and what he had to do next. He decided that having made this first step he would bring them together as an advisory group. He believed that by offering this open and transparent approach the majority would bring along the minority. What he was absolutely sure about is that he would not allow any whispering in corridors to begin. The firm was the only thing that mattered and negative influences would be dealt with swiftly.

Shirley Horn sang "Here's to Life" from his Spotify Daily Mix. He heaved a sigh. It had been a good but difficult day. But he felt that they had made a big step forward. Two texts came up on the dashboard from his phone. The first was from one of the partners from whom he had expected a lot of challenge: "Great meeting John. You have my full support. Just tell me what you want." John smiled. The second was from Vanessa: "Gone to Yoga, can you collect Livvy from school at 8:00. Back at 10:30."

Building a culture needs to become personal to the leader. He or she must lead. Process is important to scaling culture but the leader needs to reach out at the outset and engage the emotions of his or her key people in the organisation. It is like ripples in a lake and they are essential to bringing along everyone in the firm. This is an area often remote to a leader who is likely to have had no previous training in leading in this way. At this point his or her actions are far more akin to a sports coach. A sports coach cannot hide as his or her results are immediate and league tables are posted and re-posted after every game. In any culture every individual brings a unique set of attributes to the group. Pep Guardiola, currently manager of the Premier League club Manchester City, who learned and honed his skills at Barcelona FC where in the four years that he was there won 14 out of the 19 league and cup trophies available to them, said: "A team's culture is about the conduct and behaviour of everyone involved, it's working together towards shared objectives and as such, is an immediately identifiable part of the group's identity."[23]

But there will be some who possess more social influence than others. Some who because of their achievements and because of their experience will have a much greater influence on a group of people. Willi Railo, the Norwegian psychologist, called these people 'cultural architects'. These are the players who the rest of the team respect, who the rest of the team look to for leadership; the people who are able to change the mindset of others.

How the leader deals with these key people determines the success of the project. The most successful coach in the US NBA over two decades is Gregg Popovich of the San Antonio Spurs. This is based on an amazing set of statistics that show 'wins above expectation' taking account of the skills of the players to win a game. Popovich's rate of winning is more than double that of the next nearest coach. Popovich's personality is key to their success. He believes in telling it as it is and then "loving them to death". He goes to great lengths to connect with his players. He seeks to understand them, to show he cares. He genuinely loves his players, where they come from, their families, their ambitions, their needs, their challenges. "Hug 'em and hold 'em" is how he often describes it to his coaches. He will find different ways of doing it but food and drink is high up on his agenda, creating quality time to get into deep discussions with his players and, in particular, the ones whom he knows will have that greater influence on the others.

A leader in a law firm needs to think like a football or basketball coach. He or she needs to go to great lengths to draw close the cultural

"Building a culture needs to become personal to the leader. He or she must lead. Process is important to scaling culture but the leader needs to reach out at the outset and engage the emotions of his or her key people."

architects as part of the team and that can only be achieved if he or she can show that they care for them, their progress, their lives and their families. He or she cannot leave them on the outside, but if they cannot be included in his or her thinking and as leaders in his or her plans, then he or she must let them leave. Any cultural architect who is not part of the vision and who sees himself or herself on the outside is damaging to the project and will work against it.

It is likely that as a firm you will already have a set of values. In the January–February 2018 edition of *Harvard Business Review*, in "The Leader's Guide to Corporate Culture", Groysberg, Lee, Price and Cheng explore the strategic effectiveness of corporate culture and identify eight different types of corporate culture styles: caring; purpose; learning; enjoyment; results; authority; safety; and order (see https://hbr.org/2018/01/the-culture-factor).

Each of these styles is delivered by a set of behaviours in an organisation. Some styles work together and are co-dependent but many are not.

A number of these styles can co-exist and can even be supportive of each other but some are in conflict and it is up to the leader to ensure that by trying to accommodate his or her people's values that he or she doesn't inadvertently adopt values that are not supportive of each other and work against each other. It seems like common sense but often, in a desire to keep everyone happy, values conflict and the opportunity to drive a business through its culture and values are lost.

To create a business with innovation at its heart a firm needs to have learning as its main focus. This encourages both self-development – surely critical in the business life of a lawyer as he or she moves from being a technical lawyer to becoming a trusted and needed adviser to his or her clients – and also constant improvement in the firm and its services which becomes a shared obsession of everyone in the business. To be honest, it is not a difficult sell as most lawyers enjoy learning and self-improvement. The real challenge will be focusing on the behaviours which will ensure it is meaningful.

Chapter 5

Communication

It's about communication. It's about honesty. It's about treating people in the organization as deserving to know the facts. You don't try to give them half the story. You don't try to hide the story. You treat them as – as true equals, and you communicate and you communicate and communicate.
Louis V Gerstner, Jr

Of course, it is all very well having wonderful mission statements and great objectives but you are not going to create the culture that you need to inspire and motivate everyone in the business if you do not have a strong communication plan and if you are not spearheading that communication. We no longer live in a world where people will do exactly as you ask. Perhaps that is wrong. Perhaps they will but will they go the extra mile that you require? Will they provide the passion that you need to achieve what you want unless the objectives are shared and everyone believes in the aims? Will they become ambassadors for your dreams? Will they feel pride in your mission? Of course not. The answer is not money and rewards. Certainly not at this stage. They must believe in you and your vision and that you are able to lead them to achieving that vision.

At a very simple level, Robert Cialdini in his book *Influence: The Psychology of Persuasion*[24] refers to an experiment by Harvard social psychologist Ellen Langer. The premise is that when we ask people to do something for us we are more likely to be successful when we provide a reason. People like to understand and have reasons for what they do. Langer asked people waiting to use a photocopying machine: "Excuse me, I have five pages. May I use the photocopier because I'm in a rush?" Of those asked, 94% let her go ahead of them, but when she said "Excuse me, I have five pages. May I use the copying machine?", only 60% agreed.

If the reason given had been even fuller, for example, "Excuse me, I have five pages. May I use the photocopier as I'm late for my dentist appointment?", it is likely that the success rate would have been even greater.

Lawyers are often not trained as well as they could be to frame the reasons for their requests. Their approach is often adversarial. But if you want to get people on your side, if you want people to follow and to get fully behind you, then there is no doubt that you should fully frame your actions and be prepared to answer any questions or challenges.

Good leaders have large amounts of emotional intelligence. They know how to engage, how to be transparent and how to inspire and motivate. There is a language of leaders that helps them to influence to achieve results.

Inspiring leaders make us want to achieve more. They make us want to go to the office. They persuade us to their thinking and their cause. They help us to work harder, more intelligently and to work with others. They make us proud to do what we do. To do that they communicate continuously. They are creative in their communications. They show that they are listening and keep us passionately adhered to their vision. They do not avoid bad news but they help us to face it with a renewed optimism and with clear direction. They make us feel everything is possible. They may not always do what we want but they demonstrate that they have listened. They respect our views so we feel even more committed and prepared to work even harder.

They motivate at both a personal and a firm level. Both are important. It is key to the achievement of the objectives that there is a consistent optimistic message coming from the leader that we totally believe. But for those key architects it also important that they know the leader believes in them and that they are key to success. At a charity lunch I attended, Gary Neville, the ex-Manchester United and England full back, was asked about the leadership skills of Sir Alex Ferguson, possibly the greatest sports team leader of all time. He gave an example of Ferguson's skills as a leader. He said that he would take him to one side on the training pitch and he would say we are playing a particular team in a few weeks and they have a very fast, tricky winger and I need you to be at your best. As Neville said: "I didn't know whether I was the best player in the club and I was being saved for this big match or I was being dropped for the next two matches."

Good leaders think carefully about their words and their actions. The whole firm is watching how they behave and they need to work out carefully the framing of their communications and often their behaviours, which is a key part of communication.

It is much easier to be a good leader if you are your own authentic self. Working out your way of leading is much easier if it is closer to you as a person. If it is a leadership style that you are comfortable with then it will be more effective. But, like everything else, there are also lots of things to learn.

Radical transparency

The concept of radical transparency is discussed by Ray Dalio in *Principles: Life and Work* (Simon & Schuster, 2017). Achieving what you set out to achieve is easier with highly motivated teams, and to motivate a team meritocracy is the best approach. The age-old command and control approach is a thing of the past. If you can see that goals are best achieved by turning people into followers and to do that you must treat them as volunteers who have to be convinced by the power of your logic and your persuasive skills, and that your ideas or ways are best for the firm and for them, then it is very easy to take the step of allowing people to see for themselves rather than receive processed information that has clearly been doctored for their eyes. A radical openness forces issues to the surface and to be dealt with. If the future looks bleak and you are residing over a 'burning platform' then you must share every detail of that with the team. If growth and profit have flatlined, or are decreasing, and as you look to the future all you can see is cost-cutting and a reduction of investment activity in order to maintain profits, then you must share that. What better way is there to help your argument that innovation and new ideas, new markets and new clients are the way forward? What better way is there to focus the minds of everyone to look at new methods, to understand the need for change? Too often leaders believe that they should protect their people from bad news even though they are mature individuals who are used to dealing with the discouraging vicissitudes of life. Most importantly, when they are trusted they will tie themselves to the mast if at the same time you can convince them of the way out and that they are part of the change in fortunes that will come. If you can paint the big picture that your ideas will lead to, they will support you, bad news or no bad news. And they will play their part no matter what level in the organisation they are at. I recall a story of a number of upmarket country golf clubs that provided expensive *eau de cologne* to its members in the locker rooms. The cost of this over several months became prohibitive as members, quite liking this perk, would often take the bottles home with them. The cost then appeared in the management accounts and each month the directors would discuss what they could do about it, from stopping it altogether to providing a lower-cost brand. After a number of discussions one enlightened director said, "leave it with me and I'll talk to Joe". Joe was the caretaker of the locker room in one of the clubs. Over the following months it ceased to be an issue and virtually disappeared from the management accounts, falling back into budget. Joe had suggested that he removed the top from each of the bottles before he laid them out. Problem solved. It is amazing just how intelligent your people are if you ask them. Leaders do not have all the answers. They just know where to find them.

Do not misunderstand radical transparency – it does not mean total openness. There are clearly still some things that must remain confidential, such as people's personal issues, perhaps individual earnings, even merger issues, etc. But it does mean more transparency than is typical and it does mean not being afraid to show vulnerability; even showing the leader's own vulnerabilities. The leader must get the balance right between showing passion for, and belief in, his or her ideas and admitting that, because this is all new, he or she needs the help of everyone to make it possible. The leader does not have to have all the answers. Leaders need others to follow them on the journey and they must work out how to achieve that.

Communication comes in all forms; addressing the whole firm, working with small groups and working on a one-to-one basis. What leaders must remember at all times is that leaders must create leaders. Colleagues need to not only be empowered but they need to be ambassadors. The leader's aim is to create a movement that will drive change with the leader being merely the catalyst. The leader should not be simply 'in' the business but 'on' the business, each day thinking about what is required and then implementing and understanding that whatever he or she does will be scrutinised, analysed, picked apart or followed by others. The leader must be authentic otherwise whatever is achieved will be like building a house on sand which will quickly fall apart. So the leader should decide the type of leader he or she wishes to be and must be disciplined enough to be that leader on a daily basis, in and out of the office. The leader needs to understand that communication is perpetual and that a firm-wide email or webinar, for example, will quickly be discussed; in the case of emails, even forwarded and probably outside the firm. That talk at lunch to an internal focus group will soon be related to others at the photocopier or in the kitchen. Even private one-to-one conversations will be passed on. And each time this happens, a new addition or viewpoint will be added to suit the agenda of the teller. Stories develop and change. People's fear of change will add an unhelpful negative spin. However, this is not a reason to avoid communicating as it would be very easy to err on the side of less communication or to withdraw to only formal (by that I mean stuffy) communication. That will not achieve your aims. Therefore, you have no choice but to communicate, often and frequently, and it must be done consistently. It must start with the bigger picture which will always be a feature of your communication, clearly illustrating to the organisation the ambitions and goals and what success looks like. The power of your communication will be key to your success. Make it an art. Take pleasure in becoming a great communicator. Practise and learn and do not be afraid to ask for help. But if you do, ensure that you retain your authenticity and that you are true to yourself.

I have been in organisations where leaders are terrified of communication, where big discussions take place as to what information should be released. Sometimes I have heard partners say that people do not want too much information and that they just want enough to do their jobs. Some people do say that, but that does not mean it is true. It is the nature of communication that is key. It is not only financial facts, it is much more. It is the framing of the business, the good that you are doing, the culture that you are creating, where you are heading.

Paul Drechsler, former chairman and CEO of the Wates Group, one of the UK's largest construction companies said:

a decade ago I would have talked about the business in terms of sales, profit, market share and competitors. When I stand up to talk about this business now, I talk about how many jobs we have created, what we are doing to reduce our carbon footprint, and what positive effect we are having on society. We have had to broaden our storyline substantially. You've got to learn to tell your story in a way that will attract customers, attract employees and attract investment.[25]

Here are 10 principles of great communication. Great leaders and innovators use all of them at some point to a greater or lesser degree:

- Great communicators have a strong vision. They have a great sense of knowing exactly where they are heading. They have the ability to see in great detail the future of the business. Jim Collins and Jerry Porras in *Built to Last*[26] write about BHAGs. These are

"*The power of your communication will be key to your success. Make it an art. Take pleasure in becoming a great communicator. Practise and learn and do not be afraid to ask for help.*"

big hairy audacious goals and they argue that every great business has established a BHAG from a very early age. This will derive from the leader and will become the force that will drive the leader forward. The leader's driving vision through his or her passion and communication will become the vision of the business and will bring others along to share in his or her drive.

- Great communicators have great values and principles and a discipline to match. Everything begins with the leader and so it follows that to be a great leader and communicator he or she will also have strong personal values and a discipline that will ensure they stay close to their values. Discipline is key. Great leaders will want their values to be reflected in the business and will work hard to ensure that the firm not only has values appropriate to the business but that it also lives and breathes them. Every great leader will have integrity as a core value. This can mean many things to many people but at its essence it means that the leader will do what they say they will do. They will be authentic and true to their personal values. Their passion for their beliefs comes from within, it is not an act. Part of being true to themselves will be a desire to listen, learn and improve. They never accept that something is perfect and are always looking to improve. You can't be a great leader without strong personal values.

- Great communicators listen as this is key to getting support. Everyone likes to know that their opinion has been heard. People are realistic enough to know that they cannot always have their way and will trust a leader's instincts, so long as they have been heard and they are part of the conversation. The skill of a great communicator is to listen empathetically and show people that they are forming views. A good communicator should be able to use listening opportunities to show that the views of others are valued; they should also be able to challenge and change their thinking. A good leader will use what he or she has learnt and build it into their planning. Great communicators do not trample on people's thoughts and ideas but will encourage discussion and will attempt to direct it. He or she will recognise that great innovation and much momentum will come from the involvement of all. They will organise regular question and answer sessions where they are able to not only put across their vision but listen and respond to any concerns. This is a very effective process in changing people's minds.

- Great communicators keep things simple. People have a tendency to overcomplicate things. An HR director had produced a report for the board. She was called into the chairman's office. The chairman had two documents face down on his desk. He asked her which she thought was the most important document – one was about 50 pages in length and the other was about five pages. She pointed to the larger document. The chairman turned them both over: "one is your HR report" (the 50-page report) he said, "and the other is the United States Bill of Rights". In order to maintain focus and not to lose the objectives in a myriad of complexity, the leader must keep everything simple. When people around the leader create too much detail he or she needs to pull it back to its core and refocus it on a very clear vision. That does not mean that a leader should not understand the detail and all that is required to achieve the vision, it simply means that every time the leader is asked to give an opinion he or she should refer back to the essence of what the goal is. To my mind, simplicity is the greatest of the 10 principles.

- Great communicators understand that optimism is a force multiplier. Being a leader means looking, acting, walking and talking like a leader. Great leaders communicate optimism in all that they do. The way a leader looks is important. The way a leader stands is important. The way a leader talks is important. The way a leader walks is important. The way a leader listens is important. At all times he or she must exude positivity, authority and a sense of control. Leaders have doubts and concerns like everyone else.

"Great communicators prepare properly. They see every opportunity as an opportunity to get the message across and prepare accordingly. They take care with blogs and emails and practise talks until they are happy with the result."

It is important, however, even at those times that they are able to show confidence and authority.

- Great communicators use storytelling and anecdotes to convey powerful messages. Stories have the power to motivate and move people. They leave lasting impressions. They are repeated time and again and become part of folklore. They leave good examples. They are fun and interesting. They allow a leader to share part of himself or herself, to show a human side and even vulnerability. They help to win friends and followers. They become the brand. They become the product. Words sell.

- Great communicators prepare properly. They see every opportunity as an opportunity to get the message across and prepare accordingly. They take care with blogs and emails and practise talks until they are happy with the result. They understand the importance of delivery and the demonstration of authority. They will use professional help to ensure that their performance is as good as it can be.

- Great communicators understand the value of framing. This is the value of context. Everyone in the organisation will benefit from an understanding of why the organisation is doing what it is doing. Taking the organisation back to its roots, explaining why it exists and its purpose. Hopefully, this will be beyond an increase in profits per partner but will be something compelling that will make every employee or colleague proud to be part of the organisation and its *raison d'etre*. No one is interested in increasing the take home pay of the equity partners other than the equity partners. To create followers in the organisation the leader will need to frame his or her ambitions in a form that will capture their imagination and their desire to go the extra mile. How he or she frames his ambitions will determine whether he or she can inspire followers to be motivated to deliver. Author Simon Sinek refers to this as the 'golden circle'. Inspired organisations act from the inside out. They focus on why. They focus on purpose. They focus on behaviours.

Everything that Apple does involves thinking differently and challenging the status quo. Apple does not focus on revenues or even on their computers. It focuses on lifestyles – 1,000 songs in your pocket. Law firms focus on profits per partner or number of offices or number of M&A deals. Your people and your clients do not care about those things; it will not galvanise dedication and loyalty. Jack Welch, when he led GE to be the largest company in the world, said that in the first few years he focused on results and revenues. It was only when he began to focus on behaviours that, he commented, the company started to improve its revenues. Great leaders know that. A classic management story is that of the three stonecutters who are asked what they are doing. The first replies "I am making a living"; the second says, "I am doing the best job of stonecutting in the entire county"; while the third says with a twinkle in his eye, "I am building a cathedral".

- Great communicators understand the power of giving. Takers look to see what people can do for them. Givers look to see what they can do for you. Adam Grant at Wharton argues that most people are matchers – you do something for me and I will do something for you. Givers often sacrifice themselves but they make their organisations better. The chief giver in an organisation should be the leader. Adam Grant says that in every job in every organisation that he has studied the givers are the most successful – so long as they also know how to be a receiver.[27] Givers are your most valuable people and so the leader needs to promote them and protect them.

- Great communicators understand the value of philanthropy in an organisation. It was Warren Buffett who said: "If you're in the luckiest 1 percent of humanity, you owe it to the rest of humanity to think about the other 99 percent."[28] Truly it is not just our responsibility, it is our privilege and a leader that can harness and create a giving organisation through his or her leadership and communication will create an immensely powerful force.

John's story

John pulled out of his drive. Radio 4 was once again opining on Brexit. He switched quickly to the World Service. And then to Classic FM. He was stressed. The next two days were key days in his plans. It was the firm's annual away days. He was conscious that in the past these had been as much about getting everyone together, enjoyment and more of the same. This year was different. His keynote speech was all about change. It was about innovation and the need to change. He wasn't sure how it would be received. He had deliberately written his speech to show a vision of a new and exciting law firm. He would focus on the positive and the excitement and the benefits to everyone if they got it right. But he couldn't avoid the need to show how they must change. He had brought in two change specialists to lead separate sessions to show how to go about making change. He had spent a lot of time with each of them to understand their message and address how they would complement each other and his speech. He knew that there would be lots of questions and much scepticism. So he had also scheduled a number of smaller focus groups at which he and key partners would take open questions. He had thought carefully how to manage this and had been advised to seek questions before the sessions but in the end he had decided that they should not restrict the meetings in any way. The way forward, he felt, was totally honesty. They were all in this together and his leadership team didn't need to know all the answers. They needed to be secure in their lack of knowledge as they went into the unknown together and secure in their leadership as they led the firm through this challenging time. In his mind he has also scheduled lots of informal meetings with key people who he needed to be on side.

It was a bright sunny October morning. John switched on Spotify. He searched for music by John McLaughlin and decided to enjoy the drive and the moment. How good could life get? He had been given the opportunity to change his firm and in doing so the lives of so many people.

Innovative teams (1)

Innovation and new and challenging ideas will generally come out of good team dynamics. Teams need to be chosen carefully. Each team member must bring something to the process. And their contribution may need to be drawn out of them.

There is a story[29] about a former British Lions head coach, Ian McGeechan, when working with one of his teams. McGeechan understood the influence of significant individuals in a team and their ability to win a game but he knew that even more important than that was the power of the team working together, working for each other and for the team. He knew that it was his job to create that team power. He sat in front of the team with a whiteboard and pen and he asked them to shout out the assets that great teams had: "fight, support, leadership, trust, helping, going the extra mile, listening" came the responses. When there were 10 or so words on the board he asked them to grade them on a scale of 1 to 10 according to which was the most important. The consensus was that trust was the most needed asset to build a great team. McGeehan turned to the team and asked them if they trusted each other. Lots of nods. He then asked each team member to go to the person in the team that they trusted and admired most and the person they trusted and admired least, and tell them why. There were lots of uneasy shuffles. And McGeechan said, "We have a lot of work to do."

Getting teams to work together by building trust is not easy. But the reward is immense. When a team is fully supportive of everyone else in the room the meetings will be much more fun, the ideas will flow, the support for each other will be far greater and the return immense.

John's story

It had been a very long day when John left the conference centre and pressed the dial for Jazz FM. Madelaine Peyroux's vocal chords filled the sound system in the car with "Don't Wait Too Long". He listened to the first few bars but soon realised that what he really wanted was silence. The day had been difficult and he hadn't felt totally comfortable answering lots of the questions thrown at him. He knew that change would be difficult. He had read a lot about change and had tried to anticipate everything that could happen. He felt that he had created a group of strong supporters to help him and together they had created a strong vision of the future. They had gone to great lengths to communicate the vision and even to empower others to go forward with the vision. These were all steps in the change process but he felt that they had failed at the first step – showing a sense of urgency. He knew he could only do this if he could show revenue or potential revenue drop. The partners were obsessed by the firm's profits per partner figure and how it would impact on them. He needed to show declining margins, loss of clients and emerging competitors that would take their market and reduce their revenues if they didn't respond. He determined that he would put a call in to the firm's auditors in the morning to see if their consultancy arm could offer some support. He wanted informed projections that would show declining revenues and, consequently, profits per partner if they didn't face up to substantial change. Without this Armageddon scenario he knew that he couldn't succeed and they needed to hear it from someone else. They needed to hear it from an independent source. He had certainly got their attention but he hadn't done enough to change the status quo. If he was going to achieve the turnaround he wanted through innovation he was going to have to go deep into the organisation and he was going to have to hit them at an emotional level. While he was doing that perhaps he could focus his innovation ideas on a small area of the business. If he could get some results in one small area of the business perhaps he could bring with him some of the sceptical partners. At the same time they would get some necessary experience. He knew precisely the area to focus on.

But for now he was feeling a bit alone and isolated. He remembered the days when he and Vanessa would talk over supper long into the night about their day. How he would love to do that tonight. Just to share with her his anxieties. He pulled over at the off licence just around the corner from home and bought a bottle of Manzanos 1961. It was Vanessa's favourite Rioja. As he pulled in the driveway her Range Rover Evoque pulled up next to him and Vanessa lowered her window: "I'm off to Isobel's. She's having problems with Alex again" – Alex was Isobel's 15-year-old son – "she wants someone to talk to." Before he could ask what time she would be back, Vanessa had sped away. John placed the Rioja carefully in the glove compartment.

Chapter 6
Teamwork

It is one of the most beautiful compensations of this life that no man can sincerely try to help another without helping himself.
Ralph Waldo Emerson

Teamwork does not happen naturally in law firms. Lawyers are often independent practitioners. They undertake work in the main on their own and they are judged by senior partners or remuneration committees either by the number of hours that they undertake or by the size of their clients or both. It breeds insecurity and a defensiveness around a lawyer's practice. Even where lawyers work in teams on large projects, it is unusual to be trained in the exercise of project management. Lawyers are expected to develop these skills by osmosis – not easy.

Groups of people are remarkably intelligent and will be smarter together than the smartest person in them. In his book, *The Wisdom of Crowds*, James Surowiecki[30] sets out to prove the power of group intelligence both scientifically and logically. One example that Surowiecki uses is the game show "Who Wants to be a Millionaire?" where contestants are asked multiple-choice questions that get increasingly difficult and if the contestant gives 15 correct answers in a row he or she wins £1 million. If a contestant cannot answer a question then they can ask the audience or phone a friend, or have two of the multiple choice answers removed increasing the likelihood of a successful guess. Everything we believe would suggest that phoning a friend and asking an expert would be the most successful option. In fact, the experts did quite well getting it right 65% of the time. But this paled into insignificance when compared with audiences who get it right 91% of the time. Surowiecki explains that these are random groups of people who choose to spend their afternoons in tv studios because, presumably, they have nothing else to do. Harsh, but he makes his point well. Teams are very powerful.

To find, develop and, ultimately, execute innovation and grow a culture that fosters innovation requires teamwork bar none. It starts with the leader but a leader's job is to create leaders and so each of the chosen project leaders must step up to run his or her team in such a way as to maximise their results.

The leader will develop a steering committee which will determine the projects that the firm will wish to put in front of the innovation project teams. The choice of leader for each of those project teams is critical to their success. The briefing and the training of each of those leaders is essential. Often leaders will have been chosen because of their passion and enthusiasm. Providing them with the tools and the processes to enable them to succeed is key. The managing or senior partner should be doing this through a combination of such things as regular blogs and other useful tools, visiting occasional meetings, and one-to-ones.

The senior or managing partner will have worked hard to create an innovative culture and will have stated the goals that the new culture will be expected to deliver. Everything that has gone before will now be expected to be learnt by the project leaders who will deliver specific innovations that will drive the organisation forward. The project leader should choose his or her own team and should be encouraged to bring in different skills and not just friends or like-minded individuals. Challenge should be seen as a good thing that will bring about radical innovation which will help to refine and deliver winning products. The project leader should be encouraged not to shy away from or be afraid of such challenge. Before the first meeting the senior or managing partner will have sent a briefing note to his project leaders with his or her thoughts and guidelines. He or she will then meet with each of them to discuss the project, the team they have chosen and the process.

It is likely that the team will be no more than seven or eight people representing different parts of the organisation; it will include senior lawyers, junior lawyers and others, and there should be a good mix of geographical offices and perhaps gender and race. But what is most important is that the team members want to be part of and understand the value of what they are being asked to do and that they are open-minded and prepared to work hard as a part of a team. Creating and fostering a shared obsession is key to success. The founder of Patagonia, Yvon Chouinard, has many strong convictions. He has people in his organisation who care about their environment and what they can do to protect it. Just as the senior partner must choose his project leaders carefully to ensure that they share the same vision, the project leader must also choose his people carefully so that they share the same obsession. The best innovative teams become almost cult-like in their approach. The project leader is likely to be a charismatic person who will be demanding of his or her team members, in particular in between meetings. They will each have jobs to do in the firm and so much of this work for the team will be done at home and at the weekends. Their jobs are already demanding as they will still have clients to look after. The requirements from the firm at this stage are unlikely to lessen. It is also unlikely that their hourly targets will be reduced and the firm is still more likely to better reward those who do the most chargeable hours. So the leader and the project leader both need to be persuasive to convince each team member of the value of their role. They will want each of their team members to make an emotional investment in order to deliver. Successful teams will deliver results and build relationships and communication lines that will soon convince the wider firm, the board and the remuneration committees of the importance of their work. But it should

"The team must fully understand its purpose. It must understand where it is going, what is expected of it and what the time frames are, and it must determine and set its values."

not be taken for granted and treated like another meeting or project. The teams need to feel empowered, proud, motivated and enlightened and that their project will make a real difference. They need to be allowed to fail just as much as they are allowed to succeed. It is also a chance to help their own personal development and to be seen by others as potential leaders. Leaders create leaders.

The team must fully understand its purpose. It must understand where it is going, what is expected of it and what the time frames are, and it must determine and set its values. That means creating a vision for the team, communicating and living the vision. It is not something that is discussed at the first meeting but never discussed again. It should bring a daily focus to the team. A great vision for the team will not only articulate people's hopes but it will touch their hearts and spirits and help them to understand how they can contribute.

The project leader also needs to have resilience. The project will not always go smoothly and he or she must have the ability to keep it on track, to pull out of projects that are not going to succeed and at the same time have the ability to keep the morale of the team high and move forward with other projects.

At the first meeting, the job of the leader is to ensure that each member feels comfortable. There will be lots of time to set out and frame the vision and to harness their ideas. The aim of the first meeting (or meetings) is to set out the purpose and the culture and to create teamwork, in particular in large firms where the team members may not know each other. Sometimes the leader can introduce a useful exercise to encourage the members to get to know each other.

Part of that first meeting (or meetings) should be used to understand the project's aims, determine the values, set the goals, establish what is expected of the team and each individual, and settle on a process. Agreeing a set of courtesy rules will be very useful. These should be determined in a group session by the team and not delivered by the leader as an expectation. They should be very specific, such as everyone should attend all the meetings, no one should be late, the use of mobile phones should be avoided, and each team member should listen when someone else in the team is talking. The role of the leader is to help everyone to enjoy being there. Having fun and good banter is an important part of the process. In the early meetings it may be detrimental to set strict timetables in order that good discussion and a flow of ideas may be encouraged. At the same time, it is good to create a dynamism around the project that will encourage the team members to be thinking about the project in between meetings or whenever they are at their most innovative or creative – walking the dog, running, or even while having a bath. The leader would be wise to come with a set of manageable reading materials that will encourage good and creative thinking around the project. The leader's most important role at this stage is to tease out each team member's passion as to what can be achieved and the importance of that to the firm.

Rarely, unless they are football coaches, do people and leaders understand the power of teams. You are asking people to go the extra mile, to give the best of themselves and give up their time. How leaders approach the meetings so that everyone will want to be part of the challenge is critical. Try to hold meetings away from the office and, if possible, in interesting places such as colleagues' homes. Or take a walk to discuss issues, giving different groups different topics and finish at the pub to bring it all together. Create big events and make statements that are fun and will become talked about for a long time; for example, get out of town, take the train up Snowdon and walk down. The walk is easy but long and allows lots of time to pair off and discuss ideas. Most of all, make it fun. Otherwise, why should anyone bother?

John's story

John swung out of his drive. Kamasi Washington was coming out of his speakers. The volume paused as he answered the phone. He had already asked the relationship partner from the firm's auditors to come round to the office mid-morning to discuss potential scenarios regarding the financial effect on the business, in particular its profits per partner, if the firm didn't evolve or innovate. The call was to confirm the meeting.

John had also decided to create an Imagineering team, a term that he had coined from Disney. Walt Disney Imagineering (WDI) is the creative force that imagines, designs and builds all Disney theme parks, resorts, attractions and cruise ships worldwide, along with overseeing the creative aspects of Disney's games, merchandise and publishing businesses. It is the creative force behind Disney. Its unique strength comes from its diverse global team of creative and technical professionals, who build on Disney's legacy of storytelling to pioneer new forms of entertainment.

It was founded in 1952 as WED Enterprises to design and build the world's first theme park – Disneyland. It is where imagination and creativity combine with cutting-edge technology to create unforgettable experiences and products. In 2018, Imagineering expanded to include the design and development of all of Disney's consumer products, including games/apps, merchandise and publishing. It is core to Disney's approach to innovation to stay ahead of its competition.

John wanted to set up a project group to consider the various parts of the business that should be considered for innovation. He was going to invite some of the key influencers in the business but had also invited a legal futurist who could inform them of changes afoot in the law, and he was hoping they would be joined by the founder of one his entrepreneurial clients known for his approach to innovation and new ideas. He knew that this team, if it worked well, would spawn lots of innovation teams.

The automatic door of the underground garage rolled back and John drove to his named spot on the second floor. He picked up a café macchiato and was at his desk exactly 75 minutes after leaving the house.

Innovative teams (2)

At the first meeting a lot of the team will not know each other. They may not even have met. There should be a balance in the team of senior people with lots of experience, possibly garnered from different firms over a long period of time, as well as junior lawyers and executives who can bring fresh ideas and enthusiasm. Some are likely to be intimidated and will not wish to challenge the pearls of wisdom from their senior colleagues. The leader should consider introducing exercises at an early stage to help the teams to get to know each other and begin to build a rapport. One way of doing this is to get each team member to talk about themselves at the first meeting. The leader should give each team member a sheet of paper to complete covering personal details such as:

My name is ...

The department I am in is ...

I live in ...

I was born in ...

My immediate family comprises ...

I consider my strengths to be ...

Things I care deeply about are ...

Things that upset me most are ...

The thing I'd like to improve in my life in the next year is ...

My hobbies and interests are ....

When talking to me, I value ...

The real value in an exercise like this is that the most intimidating person in the room will look human.

This is a very simple exercise that will help to break the ice. It is unlikely that one exercise will be sufficient and the project leader should look to introduce a different exercise at the first few meetings with the aim of building the necessary team spirit.

The project leader needs to understand his or her role and the senior partner will need to spend as much time with each project leader as possible doing that. The project leader needs to stop thinking like a lawyer to fulfil the role successfully. He or she needs to become a group

"There should be a balance in the team of senior people with lots of experience, possibly garnered from different firms over a long period of time, as well as junior lawyers and executives who can bring fresh ideas and enthusiasm. Some are likely to be intimidated and will not wish to challenge the pearls of wisdom from their senior colleagues."

builder, a facilitator, a coach, a mentor, a listener, a questioner, an organiser, an arbiter, a diplomat, a sounding board, a project manager, and a driver. He or she needs to be non-judgemental, caring, challenging, open, dynamic, trustworthy, optimistic, funny, light-hearted, experienced, level-headed, helpful, committed to the project and capable of doing what they say they will do. The project leader does not have to have all the answers but how he or she runs the team will determine just how successful the team can be. Most of all, however, the project leader needs to create a culture of integrity within the team. A lot of time will be put into planning a project but the same level of passion should be put into executing it. People often put a moral interpretation on integrity but at its most pure it simply means that you do what you said you would do. It was Mahatma Gandhi who said: "Happiness is when what you think, what you say and what you do are in harmony."[31]

The project leader should aim to build a group that is passionate in its beliefs and aims and whose members are in harmony in its operations; a team wanting to innovate and improve, willing to go the extra mile, determined to deliver, whose members like and care for each other, who are on the project all the time with enthusiasm, optimism, resilience and who are prepared to lift the lid on their imaginations with no concern of failure but only to learn and improve. If the leader can achieve that then not only will the group succeed but perhaps he or she could come and manage my favourite football club, Manchester United. Tell them I sent you.

Without teamwork the task is much more than daunting, it is impossible. With teamwork it is not only eminently achievable, it is fun and will be fulfilling for each member. Playing in teams is the most fun you can have. Well, kind of.

When people feel special they perform beyond their wildest dreams. They will perform especially well in a team culture where that culture has been carefully fostered and nurtured. It is a myth that creativity flourishes primarily in solitude. An idea may begin with one but it will be commercialised by a team. A team will evolve it, encourage it, finesse it, bring it to fruition and deliver it. It is a moot point whether introducing rewards into the group will lead to greater success. It may work for some but not necessarily for all. What is far more important is the understanding of why people are doing what they are doing aligned with a fun and enjoyable atmosphere. Small rewards can be used to encourage enjoyment in the group. Business in many ways is no different to sport and the leader should use all of his or her skills to foster that team spirit. This could include leading from the front in meetings, individual coaching and the building of self-esteem, using games and sometimes small rewards to create a fun atmosphere or choosing the right environment to ensure a pleasant ambience in meetings.

The team may need freshening up from time to time and it is a good idea to bring in occasional fresh thinking to create an impact. This may be a person who is knowledgeable in the area of the project, or it could simply be a clear thinker who will be able to motivate the team and help members to regain their focus and clarity.

Innovative teams (3)
Creating an environment for open discussion and effective brainstorming is key to being an innovative success. Below are some key tips for running creative meetings.
- Choose the room carefully. It must be away from the office and it must have space and natural light. Try to find unique environments such as character pubs, iconic buildings, or even boats.
- Give the meeting a focus by choosing a topic carefully and sending some reading matter and some questions for everyone to think about before the meeting. Encourage your team to speak to others before the meeting to gather ideas.
- Have some very simple courtesy rules for the meeting, for example, do not interrupt if someone is talking, be polite at all times and focus on issues and not people.
- Frame the brainstorm at the outset of the meeting by outlining the issue that you are brainstorming and why it is important.

- If you have brought an expert into the meeting ask them to begin with their thoughts.
- At all times act as an encourager – do not dampen any enthusiasm.
- Make sure that you maintain the fun levels throughout. Encourage banter and do not take yourselves too seriously.
- Choose some roles for people in the room. For instance, it is good to have an energiser, that is, someone to get the team on their feet to do some stretches when the energy is ebbing. It is good to have a writer, that is, someone who will keep a short note of proceedings and, in particular, actions. A reader may also be useful, that is, someone who will make a note of the books that are referred to or quotes from people in the room. These can be circulated after the meeting. A timekeeper who will keep you to your task and will bring you back together on time when you have a break is also useful. Finally, it may be worthwhile to have someone who can tell a joke or two to help the mood from time to time. A happier team will deliver a much better result and it will be more fun.
- When you begin to brainstorm, allow a total flow of ideas. Nothing is so ridiculous that it cannot be captured on a board.
- When you have captured all your ideas then begin the process of prioritising the ones that appeal to the group the most.
- Choose three to five of the top ideas and begin to use an issue process approach to fully explore each idea. Critical appraisal is essential but only at the right time. At the wrong time it can kill an emerging idea. A lot of meetings use De Bono's six hats approach where you all look at the opportunities together and you all look at the downsides and challenges together (see www.debonogroup.com/six_thinking_hats.php). Another approach is to let the person whose idea it was take ownership. Invite them to the front and ask them to explain the idea in a processed way (eg, background information, "These are the benefits that will accrue...", "I think it

will work because...", "What we need to do is..."), then invite the group to ask simple questions to understand the issue. When everyone has asked their questions, restate the idea. Then go around the room and ask everyone to provide their thoughts, observations, experiences or suggestions while the owner of the question captures the answers. When you have done this with the three to five prioritised ideas, begin to discuss all of them while the owner of each idea reminds everyone of the observations that were made previously by the group. Brainstorming is not just about generating ideas, it is also about making judgements. It is at this stage that you begin to make judgements.

- When you bring the meeting to a close, carefully agree on the next actions to be taken. Start the meeting with good news and finish the meeting with good news.

Creativity is a process more often than it is an event. Helping people to understand how they work together as a team is key to good brainstorming. Help the team to understand that creativity is not just about coming up with new ideas. You do not have to come up with something that no one else has thought of. It can be original on different levels. It may be something that is years old but with a modern twist.

Sir Ken Robinson in his book *Out of our Minds* states the role of the leader is to form and facilitate dynamic and creative teams.[32] He advocates the bringing together of teams of people who think differently. They may be of different ages and genders or with different cultural backgrounds and experiences. The role of the leader is to ensure that everyone can collaborate so that everyone can accept every contribution that is made and to build as a team on each other's contributions. At Pixar, they call this 'plussing'.

Remember that creativity can take time to evolve. Meetings will never be as long as you need and you should ensure that the gaps between meetings are productive and useful. It is the leader's job to promote a general culture of innovation. James Clear in his book *Atomic Habits*[33] when addressing the changing and adopting of new habits says that you should not be aiming to lose weight or to run a marathon or to play a piano piece, but that you should be aiming to change your lifestyle or to become a runner or to become a pianist. In essence, changing habits is not about achieving objectives but is about changing your identity. The role of the leader is to encourage each team member to think of themselves as an innovator and not simply as someone with an objective.

It is only with great teamwork that you can deliver great innovation.

Chapter 7

To innovate or not to innovate?

Those who dream by day are cognizant of many things which escape those who dream only by night.
Edgar Allan Poe

One of the challenges that leaders face is that lawyers often do not know where to start when you ask them to innovate. Quite often they have been taught a certain way by a partner and when they become partners they continue to do the same thing. So, when asked to innovate, it is not part of their thinking and not part of their culture. This chapter will look at some of the areas in law firms that could, and perhaps should, be addressed by innovative teams.

Corporate philanthropy

Corporate philanthropy or conscience capitalism, or frankly just doing good, is one area in law that is crying out for innovation. Warren Buffett famously said: "If you're in the luckiest 1 percent of humanity, you owe it to the rest of humanity to think about the other 99 percent."[34] Painting walls and digging gardens is not enough. Sadly, many law firms believe that by doing so they are making a real difference. If you really want to make a difference and if you really want to engage your people then you need to be much more innovative and creative. The good news is that it has been proven time and again that businesses in which employees are more engaged are likely to be at least 20% more productive. This is an area that can have a direct impact on the firm as a great place to work and can create an excitement and buzz within the firm. Purpose-driven companies are happier places to work and are more financially successful. Moreover, law firms are intermediaries in business with large client bases that are able to exercise much influence and make a real difference to the deep problems our societies still face. Corporate philanthropy is a growing movement. Companies do not operate or exist in isolation from the society around them. The more social improvement a company seeks, the more it will lead to economic benefits for the company. Social and economic goals are not in conflict but are integral to a company's growth.

Michael Porter, the Harvard professor and possibly the world's leading authority on competition, has argued consistently that philanthropy is good for a business.[35] It can provide a business with a competitive edge and as a result it is sustainable. Timpson, the high street key cutters, has a workforce where over 10% of their operators are ex-convicts. Chief Executive, James Timpson, argues that they do this because it is good for their business and that the recruitment landscape for ex-convicts is less competitive than elsewhere. Toms, the footwear retailer, provides a free pair of shoes for a third-world child for every pair purchased. Many others have followed this model. It is not beyond imagination to determine philanthropic policies that are good for a business.

According to Porter, there is no inherent conflict between improving competitive context and making a sincere commitment to bettering society.[36] There is nothing wrong in undertaking strategic philanthropy. In fact, it makes eminent sense for a business. But most businesses give it no thought and leave it to a low-level part of the business to run marathons and undertake sponsored walks in memory of someone who has been lost to a member of the firm, or to paint a room in a local hospice which has probably been painted five times in the last five years. This is not intended to decry the good intentions of anyone undertaking those tasks but shows the lack of strategic leadership and innovation to consider how to have real influence and make a major difference while benefiting the business at the same time.

Porter talks about businesses playing to their strengths.[37] Again, this is sensible but is often ignored. When did lawyers become decorators, for example? I certainly never acquired that skill.

But lawyers can also be influential and should not be afraid of thinking big and leading the way on major issues that society needs to address.

When did we decide that looking after the disadvantaged was the job of government? When did we abdicate responsibility for looking after those around us who are struggling, the homeless in our streets, the lonely in our communities, the aged who have given so much to us, the mentally and physically challenged who cannot help themselves, the refugees mourning the loss of loved ones, and all those without the same opportunity as we had who, because of that lack of opportunity, make bad decisions? We are tied together by our shared existence in this amazing world because "there but for the grace of God go I". Many of these disadvantages are an accident of birth. A combination of unfortunate incidents that have produced the person with whom we now share our world and our communities. What gives us the right to reject any one of them? We are citizens of the world and owe the world. What gives us the right to lay responsibility for caring for them, for supporting them, on a government or on a political system that is bureaucratic and inefficient and often inept, and will always struggle to deliver at the coalface what is needed to bring about change and to make a difference?

We continue to fight the battle against racism and sexism which rightly dominates the media but it is easy to argue that we have not yet picked up the yoke of poverty and affluence inequality. We seem very happy to live in a society where the affluent get better healthcare, where the rich can go to better schools and get a better education, and where the rich live in better neighbourhoods. These are the battles that are still to be fought and they are the hardest of all because many people benefit from such advantages, and will defend their right to do so. And this is just in the developed countries. In the United States and Europe things have always seemed more fair but this is only superficially so. Those who have graduated from the best schools with the best grades have a better chance of getting the best jobs. But the system is stacked in favour of affluent parents who send their children to the best primary schools, grammar schools and public schools. And because of our self-interest we are prepared to accept it, even if we know it is wrong and even if we know that it conflicts with our values.

To those who are given much, much is expected. Where are the heroes? Are we ready and able to take on that mantle – that responsibility of putting ourselves aside and fighting for the rights of our brothers and sisters who have suffered so much and will continue to suffer? Do we have it within us?

Do we learn nothing from history and our forefathers and mothers? Or are we so self-centred and hedonistic that we just do not care? Have we become numb to the news, to advertising and documentaries, to the vast tracts of writing, to charities' self-sacrificial endeavours and NGOs' pursuit of right and elimination of wrong? Are we not ashamed of burying our heads in the sand, in our own superficial existence? Was it not Martin Niemöller, the German Lutheran priest, who wrote:

First they came for the communists and I did not speak out because I was not a communist. Then they came for the socialists and I did not speak out because I was not a socialist. Then they came for the trade unionists, and I did not speak out because I was not a trade unionist. Then they came for the Jews, and I did not speak out because I was not a Jew. Then they came for me and by that time no one was left to speak up.[38]

How are we to live with ourselves if we turn our heads away, turn over the tv channel or turn to the sports pages because reality is too distressing to face up to? Should we ignore our values? Surely our response should be to do something – whatever it is that we can do – just something.

The Victorian philanthropists chose to respond in the only way you can, by taking action. As Joan Baez once said, "action is the antidote to despair".[39] There were bodies established to meet every conceivable need: charities for the poor, the sick, the disabled, the unemployed, the badly-housed, charities for the reclamation of prostitutes and drunkards, for reviving drowning persons, for apprentices, shop girls, cabbies, costermongers, soldiers, sailors and variety artistes. Sir James Stephen wrote in 1850: "For the cure of every sorrow ... there are patrons, vice-presidents and secretaries ... For the diffusion of every blessing ... there is a committee."[40]

Individuals took up the baton of improving the world: Florence Nightingale, Dr Barnardo, Lord Shaftesbury, Octavia Hill (the housing reformer), General Booth of the Salvation Army, Angela Burdett of Coutts Bank, George Cadbury, William Lever, Joseph Rowntree, Arthur Guinness – the list goes on. What is significant is that many of them built major profitable businesses yet what they are remembered for is social reform. Their legacy is the social reform that they led. Surely every one of us has a responsibility to leave this world in a better place than we found it, otherwise what is it all for? And from those who have achieved much and who have benefited much, and who are in positions of leadership or great influence, then much should be expected. This should be the expectation. It should be the bar by which they are judged.

Whose responsibility is poverty? Whose responsibility is it to look after the disadvantaged? Whose responsibility is it to watch over and care for those in need? We have given this responsibility to government but it just does not seem to work. Every new prime minister paints a picture of a truly utopian society. Every prime minister fails to create such an outcome. We could, I am sure, go so far as to say that every leader of every democratic country offers the same. The intentions are good, but achievement is limited. Paper after paper is produced. Committee after committee is established. Such efforts almost always lead to failure whether because of bureaucracy, conflicts of interest, too many stakeholders or the cost of investment. Programmes such as 'War on Poverty' which was designed to deliver a great society in the 1960s, New Labour and its equality rhetoric, Cameron's Big Society and Beatrice Webb's Minority Report on the Poor Law in 1909 all failed.

Whose responsibility is it? The common answer appears to be – all of us. But that does not provide focus and does not acknowledge our weaknesses or play to our strengths. It just leaves too much to chance. If you carry on doing things the same way, then you will undoubtedly get the same results.

So which part of our society is best placed to deliver results?

Apple's market value is greater than the gross domestic product of almost every country on Earth apart from about 19. There are 195 countries in the world. If WalMart were a country it would be equal to the GDP of the 25th largest country in the world. Even countries such as New Zealand, Norway and Thailand are beaten on revenue by these companies. Yahoo is bigger than Mongolia. Visa is bigger than Zimbabwe. Amazon is bigger than Kenya. Chevron is bigger than the Czech Republic and Berkshire Hathaway is bigger than Hungary... and the list goes on.

Even more interesting are the SME statistics. An SME is a company that employs fewer than 250 people. In the United Kingdom, figures from the Department of Business, Innovation and Skills in 2015 show that there are an estimated 5.4 million private sector businesses employing 15.6 million people with a turnover of £1.8 trillion. Larger businesses employ 10.3 million people with a turnover of £2 trillion. And all are led by a CEO or a founder. It is these talented achievers from whom much is expected. To whom much is given, much is expected. It is to these successful over-achievers that we must now turn. It is these influencers that we must support and encourage, that we must recognise and nudge to even greater achievements. Achievements that will deliver a utopian society. And our professional firms can do a lot to lead the way. Lawyers

"Whose responsibility is it to watch over and care for those in need? We have tried government and it just does not seem to work. Every new prime minister paints a picture of a truly utopian society. Every prime minister fails to create such an outcome."

– whatever jokes are made of them – have a lot of integrity and are held in high regard. Their professionalism and thoroughness are admired by many. Therefore, our professionals are well placed to show leadership in this area. Lawyers are eloquent, clever people with integrity and a large network of CEOs and entrepreneurs.

CEOs and entrepreneurs are action orientated which is the reason for their success. Entrepreneurs in particular do not feel restricted by unnecessary rules and regulations. They are rarely compromised by politics. Obstacles are there to be overcome. George Bernard Shaw is believed to have said something like: "those who can, do, and those who can't, teach". I would have loved to have asked his view of politicians, journalists, critics and civil servants. But our business leaders cannot afford the luxury of endless and often meaningless debates. To do so would mean a slow death to their business as they watch it disappear. They constantly fight against the red tape imposed by bureaucrats or the often-entitled attitude of their workforce. Their greatest strength is to make decisions that will drive their business forward. To many it is like a game, a sport where the goal is to outperform the competition. Rather than fight the very virtues that they bring we should embrace them and direct them to supporting our communities. We should celebrate their dynamism, encourage it and reward it for the good it can do, for the efficiencies they show us, and the success they can bring to developing social businesses and addressing social needs. These are our heroes – not our sports stars, or celebrities, or our politicians or civil servants but men and women who know how to overcome obstacles. They are stoics who see opportunity when others see crisis. Where many see negativity, they have a vision. When many give in to feelings, they choose not to. When others see comfort zones, they question what a comfort zone is. They do not fear failure. The only failure to them is not trying. They carry hope in their hearts and where others perceive doubt and introspection they see blue oceans of success and achievement. It is these people that we want helping our communities, especially those communities whose members lack the same good fortune as ourselves. These are our heroes. It is a time for heroes.

Entrepreneurs and business leaders are uncompromising in their quest to build a successful business. They have had to be. The profit-driven model means without that drive they face extinction. Even to stand still is not sufficient. Jack Welch, former chairman and CEO of GE, claimed that if you stand still, you watch your competitors pass you by. It takes years of dedication and unimaginable hard work, a stoical approach to overcoming obstacles and a sheer relentlessness year on year to create a winning business. It needs both a selfishness in focus and attitude, and an incredible selflessness in looking after those you have chosen to share the journey with. Without these followers a leader is just "taking a walk". Followers will no longer follow because they are directed to. They demand that their leaders earn their respect and their right to lead. Leaders in turn can only do this if they truly care for their people. Most importantly, leaders of businesses thrive on responsibility. Tim Grover, renowned for his work with elite athletes, in his book *Relentless: From Good to Great to Unstoppable* describes the very best of these as Cleaners. Cleaners, he says, are found in all walks of life. They are never content with what they have achieved. They will always push for more:

Being a Cleaner has almost nothing to do with talent. Everyone has some degree of talent; it doesn't always lead to success. Those who reach this level of excellence don't coast on their talent. They're completely focused on taking responsibility and taking charge, whether they're competing in sports or managing a family or running a business or driving a bus; they decide how to get the job done and then they do whatever is necessary to make it happen. These are the most driven individuals you'll ever know, with an unmatched genius for what they do: they don't just perform a job, they reinvent it. I own this.[41]

It is these people we need to turn to in order to change our world, to challenge the inbuilt inequalities of global citizenship. It is these people we need to find, nudge and encourage. It is these people we need to laud. These are our heroes. It is their time.

The first time we saw these Cleaners making a difference was when the Victorian philanthropists came to the fore. The progress of the industrial revolution brought under the microscope the treatment of the workforce and the general population but it was a long time before a government moved its focus to the introduction of the welfare state. The People's Budget of 29 April 1909 was the culmination of years of debate on the redistribution of wealth. Churchill and Lloyd George worked in tandem as great social reformers, with Churchill promoting the Trades Board Bill in 1909 designed to help low-paid workers. Explaining in the House of Commons why the bill was necessary, Churchill stated:

It is a national evil that any class of her Majesty's subjects should receive less than a minimum wage in return for their utmost exertions. It was formerly supposed that the working of the laws of supply and demand would naturally regulate or eliminate that evil. The first clear division that we make on the question today is between healthy and unhealthy conditions of bargaining … where you have what we call sweated trade, you have no organization, no parity of bargaining, the good employer is undercut by the bad, and the bad employer is undercut by the worst.[42]

But it is our professionals and our law firms who can play an enormous role in the education of our CEOs and entrepreneurs and who can act as role models in driving the change that is needed. This can be done by undertaking and delivering projects that make a real difference, and working with CEOs and entrepreneurs as clients to develop their thinking and direct their extraordinary abilities to make things happen for the common good and for greater equality. This should be aimed at the less fortunate, those with fewer opportunities, so that we may live in a better world. George Bernard Shaw wrote: "I hear you say 'Why?' Always 'Why?' You see things; and you say 'Why?' But I dream things that never were; and I say 'Why not?'".[43] Why shouldn't your firm be the one to take a leading role in galvanising leaders and entrepreneurs into delivering a better world?

Being a philanthropic firm means acting and thinking differently. There are something like 165,000 charities in the United Kingdom and about 1% to 2% of them account for over 70% of funding. The other 98%

are full of passionate and driven individuals aiming to do good. They could do good faster if they had the help of a visionary law firm behind or alongside them. Many of the people working in these charities have made great sacrifices because of the cause they stand for. Many could be earning much bigger salaries and living more luxurious lifestyles. None, on their salaries alone, would be able to put their children through private schooling or pay for private health insurance, or live in large houses in the affluent greenbelt. And yet they do what they do, often working harder than overworked professionals (usually working unsocial hours because in the business of saving or improving lives, time does not wait) without any grumbling, and will find pleasure in small successes. They often give the gift of life but at their own expense. Digging gardens and painting walls pales into insignificance, but we can make a real difference and we can be role models for change.

Following Porter's examples, law firms are the perfect businesses in which to grow and train teams of mentors. A joint research venture by Harvard, Stanford and Chicago universities shows that a key ingredient for good work to take place is good mentorship. Anyone can mentor with some basic training and can make a difference to those who are on the wrong side of opportunity. To mentor we do not need to be wise, we just need to care and to show or teach by our good example. Sometimes it is a matter of building self-esteem or building confidence and showing a person that someone believes in them. The fact is that as a mentor you could be a unique person in someone's life. As lawyers, at some point along the way we will have been lucky – and that luck has got us where we are. When you have the opportunity to ignite someone else's life, you do not know where it might lead but it is an opportunity you must take.

It is easy not to get involved and to convince ourselves that we are too busy or that we have others that rely on us – children, parents, friends. But we know that is our own self-justification and it is not reality.

Martin Luther King Jr, the great American civil rights leader said:

I say to you this morning that if you have never found something so clear

"As leaders and as innovators we have the chance to lead people in ways that will not only benefit our businesses but will benefit our whole world. We would be failing if we did not grasp it."

and so precious to you that you will die for it, then you aren't fit to live. You may be 38 years old as I happen to be, and one day some great opportunity stands before you and calls upon you to stand up for some great principle, some great issue, some great cause. And you refuse to do it because you are afraid. You refuse to do it because you want to live longer. You are afraid that you will lose your job or you are afraid that you will be criticised or that you will lose your popularity, or afraid that someone will stab you or shoot at you or bomb your house. So you refuse to take the stand. Well you may go on and live until you are 90, but you are just as dead at 38 as you would be at 90. And the cessation of breathing in your life is but the belated announcement of an earlier death of the spirit. You died when you refused to stand up for right. You died when you refused to stand up for truth. You died when you refused to stand up for justice ... [44]

As leaders and as innovators we have the chance to lead people in ways that will not only benefit our businesses but will benefit our whole world. We would be failing if we did not grasp it. As King said:

And I am simply saying this morning that you should resolve that you will never become so secure in your thinking or your living that you forget the least of these ... In some sense all of us are the least of these. I try to get it over to my children, early, morning after morning, when I get a chance. As we sit at the table, as we did this morning, in morning devotions. I couldn't pray my prayer without saying "God help us as we sit at the table to realise that there are those who are less fortunate than we are. And grant that we will never forget them no matter where we are". And I said to my little children "I'm going to work and do everything I can to see that you get a good education. I don't ever want you to forget that there are millions of God's children who will and cannot get a good education, and I don't want you feeling that you are better than they are. For you will never be what you ought to be until they are what they ought to be". [45]

There are many ways that a business and a law firm can be innovative in the field of corporate philanthropy, play to the firm's strengths and at the same time provide the business with a competitive edge. But if that is not enough, do it because, as King says, it is the right thing to do. We are no better than anyone else and we should be prepared to help those who have not been as lucky as we have.

It may be taking a leadership role and working with some key clients or clients that you would like to work with. Imagine the benefit of that to your business. Or it may be developing a professional mentoring programme with your people. Imagine the effect of that and the engagement with your staff when you share the good news stories. Or it may be joining up with a charity and undertaking a key project on its behalf. Charities often look to law firms to raise funding from sponsored activities, but why not take the extra step and run events for them? Whatever it is that you choose to do, ensure that it is strategic and benefits the business as it will then be sustainable. Ensure that the whole leadership team is behind it and align it to the purposes of the business.

The first rule

The first rule is that clients come first. The second rule is that there is no second rule. So if you are considering innovative ways to improve your business then service to your clients must be at the top of the list. It was in 1985 that *The American Lawyer* first published profits per partner and that has become the key driver of every major law firm. It is hard to see just exactly how clients come first in a model that is more concerned with profits per partner. To focus solely on profits per partner is a short-lived strategy. To attract, secure, maintain and develop quality clients requires a process and system that ensures the delivery of a consistently high quality of service right across your practice. It is in effect a Total Quality Management System. Clients need to feel that they are your most important client. Any innovation programme would be failing if one of the major projects was not client service. If you can instil throughout your business a culture of client service and great client experiences then you will not need to invest in advertising because clients will do it for you.

What most lawyers think of as client service is what most clients believe is expected and even basic. When you book into a hotel room you require certain basic things – a bed, some clean sheets on the bed, pillows etc. Other things may not be basic but are expected. These might include a television, *en suite* facilities, nice toiletries or a minibar. The key word is 'expected'. These are not the things that bring a customer back time and time again for life. Customers return because of the 'wow' factor. A while ago as I left a hotel the doorman hailed a taxi for me. Twenty minutes later, after I had got out of the taxi, I realised that I had left my phone on the seat. There was that inevitable sinking feeling. I called the hotel with forlorn hope. The concierge was magnificent – he took my details, chased down the taxi, found my phone, retrieved it and put it in the post to me. Do you think I will go back to that hotel? You bet I will. Do you think I will go back for life? It will take something truly magnificent to entice me away. Compare that to a few months ago when staying at a hotel and leaving my phone charger in the phone socket – something I appear to do on a regular basis, sadly. As soon as I left the hotel and realised my loss I called the hotel and spoke to the receptionist who very politely said that they would check the room (expected) and who returned my call (expected) to tell me that it was not there. That was it. What a missed opportunity! Why could someone not think to buy a new charger for a minimal sum and send it to me in the post? Imagine the wow factor in that. Imagine the lifetime of loyalty they could have achieved.

Exceptional client service is rare. Creating a 'wow' factor all the time is even rarer.

Ask anyone in the retail industry what the first words are that come to their mind when they think of Nordstrom, and they will immediately tell you 'customer service'. Making your brand synonymous throughout an industry, in particular a service industry, in this way is quite an achievement. It has taken over a century for Nordstrom to achieve this, but stories about the upscale fashion retailer are now legendary.

It has taken Nordstrom 115 years of complete dedication to create the finest shopping experience to build such a reputation. The secrets of its success are set out in Spector and Reeves's *The Nordstrom Way to Customer Experience Excellence: Creating a Values-Driven Service Culture* (Wiley, 2017).

Nordstrom's exceptional customer service is, primarily, the result of two main factors: 1) attention to detail when it comes to customer experience; and 2) the level to which employees are empowered.

These two factors together result in a relentless customer service engine that continues to generate stories that perpetuate the legends around Nordstrom.

A former employee gave an insight to some of the thinking at Nordstrom:

- *A Nordstrom salesperson rarely points. If you have a question about where something is located, they walk you there.*
- *Salespeople are taught to walk your bagged purchases around the counter and hand to you versus just handing it across the counter.*
- *Salespeople can offer to ring up your purchase without you ever having to stand in line. This particularly happens a lot in the shoe departments.*
- *Departments are generally trained to answer the phone on no more than the second ring.*

Source: www.quora.com/Why-is-Nordstrom-known-for-their-good-customer-service

These are traditional shopper 'pain points' that Nordstrom goes out of its way to eliminate when you shop in its stores.

It is clear from these answers that Nordstrom has carefully designed its client service and then gone to great trouble to ensure it is executed well.

One of the challenges that law firms face is that training is almost always about technical service and clients do not become an obsession in the same way. In fact, clients are often seen as an intrusion. Bizarre but true. Chris Daffy in his wonderful book *Once a Customer, Always a Customer*[46] writes that while our business schools and management training programmes graduate people who can read a balance sheet or understand statistical analysis, many of these graduates do not understand that it is customers – not products or services – that are the only source of sales, profit, growth and anything else that matters to a company. He shares in his book a list of 10 golden rules:

Customers are:

- *the most important people in any business;*
- *not dependent on us – we depend on them;*
- *not an interruption of our work – they are the purpose of it;*
- *doing us a favour when they call – we do not do them a favour by serving them;*
- *part of the business – not outsiders;*
- *not a cold statistic but flesh and blood human beings with feelings and emotions like our own;*
- *not someone to argue or match will with;*
- *people who bring us their wants – our job is to satisfy them;*
- *deserving of the most courteous and attentive treatment we can provide;*
- *the life blood of every business.*

Source: Chris Daffy, Once a Customer, Always a Customer, (Oak Tree Press, 2011)

Developing an obsession about client service and really believing it is key to any innovation and its success. Vernon Hill, the founder and chairman of Metro Bank, has written a book entitled *Fans not Customers*.[47] The premise of the book is that there are customers and there are fans. Customers are those people who come in, who do their banking at Metro but who are almost indifferent to the company. They could be anywhere. It is a convenience model. Hill says that they start out being absolutely indifferent but the job of his employees is to convert them to becoming fans. Fans are customers who embrace your model and your culture but who also become part of your community and convert their friends to becoming customers. They become ambassadors. They want evangelists for the brand. When their friends complain about their bank, they direct them to Metro for a better service. And just like Nordstrom, stories about the company's customer service have developed. It is not just about the company allowing and encouraging people to bring their dogs into the bank or opening before they say they will, or having no steps into the branches so that people can come in with bikes; it is also about the personal stories that people tell that then become fixed in folklore just as in Nordstrom. In *Fans Not Customers*, Hill says it is all down to culture. He uses the acronym AMAZE to demonstrate their success:

A – *Attend to every detail*

M – *Make every wrong, right*

A – *Ask if you're not sure, bump it up (take it to a supervisor and decide together)*

Z – *Zest is contagious, share it*

E – *Exceed expectations*

Source: Vernon Hill, Fans not Customers *(Profile Books, 2012)*

Hill argues that successful client-faced businesses such as his always look at things from the customer's point of view. Put yourself in the customer's shoes and do not hide behind rules. His biggest challenge, he says, as they grow and recruit at increasingly faster rates is teaching bankers to unpick what they have learned elsewhere. They have a consistent Net Promoter Score score of over 80. That is deemed to be world-class.

But it begins with your people. Daffy says if you do not care about your internal customers (your staff) they will not care about your external customers. They will be incapable of providing good external customer service if they are not receiving excellent internal customer service.

Having a greater degree of empathy for your clients will enable you to

"Fans are customers who embrace your model and your culture but who also become part of your community and convert their friends to becoming customers. They become ambassadors. They want evangelists for the brand."

see and solve problems that you previously might never have noticed before. One of the most widespread anecdotes about Nordstrom relates to it having the shortest ever employee handbook:

Rule #1: Use best judgement in all situations. There will be no additional rules.

Perhaps compare that to your own handbook or the handbooks of companies that you know with pages of rules and directions about things that you can or cannot do. The bureaucracy that becomes like turgid treacle to wade through. You will then realise the emphasis that Nordstrom puts on trusting its people.

What this results in are unheard of stories from the folklore of customer service, as well as employees who feel motivated and part of an amazing, giving organisation. Nordstrom even has an elite 'million dollar club' where the top employees bring in more than a million dollars a year to the company. Part of that success is that they are encouraged to make use of client lists and to build and develop personal relationships with customers. Customer service is always personal. At Nordstrom this is not only encouraged but also taught, such as the sending of handwritten thank you notes.

When your employees are happy and are empowered then stories such as those below become commonplace.

The search for the lost diamond wedding ring

A woman in North Carolina recently lost the diamond from her wedding ring while trying on clothes at a Nordstrom store. A store security worker saw her crawling on the sales floor under the racks. He asked what was going on, then joined the search.

After they came up empty, the employee asked two building-services workers to join the search. They opened up the bags of the store's vacuum cleaners, where they found the shiny diamond.

Source: Seattle Times, www.seattletimes.com/business/tale-of-lost-diamond-adds-glitter-to-nordstroms-customer-service/.

The case of the 'rainy boots'

Do you know who's legally responsible if a common carrier (UPS, DHL, FedEx) leaves your Nordstrom delivery in the rain and your $200 shoes are ruined? Well, the responsible party might be you or it might be the trucking company, but it's absolutely not Nordstrom.

Yet, when this happened to me, not for an instant did my salesperson (the great Joanne Hassis at the King Of Prussia Nordstrom, by the way) consider saying "You need to file a claim with the trucking company". She instead told me, without hesitation, the following: "I'm so incredibly sorry that happened, and I'm bringing over a brand new pair of shoes – will you be home in forty-five minutes?"

Source: Forbes, www.forbes.com/sites/micahsolomon/2014/03/15/the-nordstrom-two-part-customer-experience-formula-lessons-for-your-business/#4c44458b445f.

The tyres story

In 1975 a man returned to a store in Alaska with four snow tyres in the bed of his truck. He bought the tyres at a tyre shop several weeks before, and he needed to return them. But as he pulled up to the supposed-to-be tyre shop where he purchased his tyres, he discovered the tyre shop was closed, and a Nordstrom was in its place. Most of us would assume the guy put his tyres into the back of his truck and drove away disappointed and frustrated about losing his money on a set of faulty tyres. But, nope. That's not what happened. We'll cut to the chase: after explaining his situation to a sales clerk, Nordstrom (a store that doesn't sell tyres, mind you) allowed him to return the tyres, AND they refunded his money.

Source: https://sharpencx.com/blog/nordstrom-customer-service/.

You might baulk at the thought of refunding such an expensive purchase, especially for items that cannot be resold. However, if you ignore the small financial blow from the equation we are left with one amazing truth – 43 years later, people are still telling this story. A lot of people, actually.

If you google Nordstrom tyres, you get roughly 1,680,000 results. There are blog posts, forum threads and news articles dedicated to the story. That single, phenomenal customer service story gave Nordstrom decades of free publicity and word-of-mouth advertising. It is a legendary customer service story, and it is owned by Nordstrom. If you are sceptical about whether it is true, several Nordstrom officials – and a book about Nordstrom – say otherwise, but even if it is folklore what a wonderful folklore that people are true evangelists about the business.

John Nordstrom puts the Nordstrom obsession better than anyone[48]: *Our commitment is 100-percent to customer service. We are not committed to financial markets, we are not committed to real estate markets, we are not committed to a certain amount of profit. We are only committed to customer service. If we make a profit, that's great. But customer service is first. If I'm a salesperson on the floor and I know that the people who own this place are committed to customer service, then I am free to find new ways to give great customer service. I know that I won't be criticised for taking care of a customer, I will only be criticised for not taking care of a customer.*

Nordstrom is testimony to the importance of empowering employees and supporting the policies that empower them to do what's best for customers. Many other companies have followed this approach and many haven't. You quickly see the difference. Nordstrom employees have the wiggle room they need to make snap decisions that benefit their customers. And they can unapologetically make those decisions without feeling like they have overstepped the mark or have no authority. Going above and beyond to take care of customers is expected, encouraged, and praised above all else.

Nordstrom does not rely on flashy sales events to entice shoppers into its stores, or constant marketing. There are occasional sale events as a loyalty incentive for Nordstrom cardholders, sure, but people go there because they can count on the service. Nordstrom is not the cheapest but people will pay for the service they know that they will receive.

It is all very interesting and of course it is great to read but how do we translate it and convey these ideas to a traditional industry such as the law? Lawyers for some reason attribute service to a sales process and believe that they are above that. Somehow, being a lawyer seems to have attracted more kudos than being a service provider. The reality is, of course, that before we are lawyers we are service providers. Our purpose should not be to deliver legal services but to deliver peace of mind. Clients approach a lawyer because they have a problem or face a challenge. They are not interested in the contract you promise – they just want you to give them peace of mind. To some extent all companies are service companies in that they create value for customers through the performance of services. Manufacturers and goods retailers are hybrid organisations in that they create customer value with a combination of goods and services. But law firms, just like hotels and airlines and medical practices, are pure service companies in that they create value almost exclusively through performances. Retailers add value to their product through services. Lawyers are the product. So it is far more important than it is to Nordstrom or to Apple that the service they provide has a 'wow' factor attached to it.

The big challenge when innovating around this area in the law is that lawyers do not see themselves as service providers and do not even see the benefits. But to move through the prism of law you have to move from being a good technical lawyer (expected), to one that adds value to the service, to one that adds value to the business, to a lawyer who becomes a trusted adviser who the client will always turn to and, finally, to a personal adviser to a client where the client will not do anything without speaking to you. The benefits in achieving this are phenomenal and result in a client who will:

- treat you as you wish to be treated;
- accept your advice more readily without and will follow your recommendation;
- be more open and involve you in all matters;
- bring you in earlier and involve you in more complex matters because they will value your judgement;

"It is not surprising that people would generally prefer to work in a company that has a brand that is recognised for providing high levels of client service than one that does not. It is more fun, less stressful and feels good to be part of."

- pay your bills without challenge;
- refer others to you and become your best ambassador;
- defend you if others should criticise you;
- become a friend;
- create satisfaction.

And in the business you will get improvements in morale which will reduce staff costs and lower staff turnover, give longer client retention and more repeat business, and the client will pay more. And what does all that lead to? A business to be proud of. So it is worth the effort.

A favourite lawyer's phrase that I have always wanted to use but have rarely had the opportunity is *res ipsa loquitur* (the thing speaks for itself). It is not surprising that people would generally prefer to work in a company that has a brand that is recognised for providing high levels of client service than one that does not. It is more fun, less stressful and feels good to be part of. And as a result people become more productive which, of course, leads to increased client retention. Research shows that clients tend to stay 50% longer. Try converting that to pounds, shillings and pence. And if that is the case then it also follows that it will lead to more repeat business. There are three ways that a lawyer can increase his or her revenues – more work from the same clients, pushing up prices and finding new clients. As well as higher retention and more work from the same client, excellent client service companies have higher margins and stronger referral systems.

Imagine all those companies that you consider provide excellent client service – for example, Apple, John Lewis, Harrods – and then consider their financial performance compared with their competitors.

The Profit Impact of Marketing Strategy (PIMS) database has been operating for some 30 years. It is a database that looks for a connection between business profitability and marketing strategies. The correlation between profitability and service levels shows the better the service levels, the better the return on investment and the better profit on sales.

A nice story

In May 2011 a three-year-old girl wrote to UK supermarket, Sainsbury's, saying that one of their products 'tiger bread' should be renamed: "Why is tiger bread called tiger bread? It should be called giraffe bread. Love from Lily Robinson age 3½". She received a reply from a customer service agent that said: "I think renaming tiger bread giraffe bread is a brilliant idea – it looks more like the blotches on the giraffe than the stripes on a tiger doesn't it? It is called tiger bread because the first baker who made it a long time ago thought it looked stripey like a tiger. Maybe they were a bit silly." The letter was signed "Chris King (age 27⅓)".

Source: www.bbc.co.uk/news/business-16812545.

This story has been seen by millions of people through Facebook and was shown on BBC news. Most of the comments were hugely positive to Chris King and the Sainsbury's brand. Sainsbury's were quick to capitalise and rename tiger bread 'giraffe bread'. Imagine the positive effect on revenues.

Creating a great client experience will create a happy and financially successful business. If you focus on delighting your client then profit becomes a well-earned by-product. It is amazing just how successful you can become when you focus on good behaviours.

But lawyers need to realise that not only is service a far greater differentiator than competent technical service which is to be expected; there is now a natural tendency to compare products and services with all those that have set standards high, not just direct competitors. We do not care if one online grocery shopping site is better than another; if the site is not as good as Amazon's we will be disappointed. If Apple, the biggest company in the world, can manage to answer the phone with a real person then why can't my bank? The bar for customer experience is no longer set by direct competitors, it is set by the experiences that we have in our day-to-day lives. Social media is also empowering the customer and though lawyers may think that they are immune to it, they are not.

So where does innovation begin when looking at client services?

Innovation is the act or process of looking at new ideas, processes or methods. In Nordstrom innovation is the value that guides the company to relentlessly seek processes and tools to better serve across all channels. Nordstrom believes that no organisation can sustain itself unless it is in a constant state of innovation and adaptation. If innovation is in the client experience field then the team leading it needs to be client obsessed. Technology is just a part and we will come to that later but it is not the panacea of all ills as many commentators seem to portray it.

Your company should not be the same company that it was five years ago and will not be the same company in five years' time. Innovation comes in many forms and it is important to break down the many client touchpoints and consider just how each can be improved. You should always be asking 'what next?'. The following are some questions that you can consider when reviewing client service.

- How easy is it to become a client?
- How welcoming are you to new clients?
- How are new clients introduced to the key people working on their matters?
- How good is your client service training?
- How good is your communication with clients?
- How good are your client events? How at home are your clients made to feel when they attend?
- How good is the client experience when they visit your offices?
- When did you last run a focus group with your clients?
- How well do your people know your clients?
- How do your people talk about clients?
- Do you have good policies on the use of mobile phone messages, taking calls and availability, and communications, both written and verbal?
- How good are your complaint policies?

Frankly, the list is endless. Why is that? Because client service is an obsession.

Pricing for adults

There were two things that always bothered me about billing by the hour. At my previous law firm billing by the hour placed a cap on my earnings. And second, I hated situations where I had won a case and I knew the other guy was getting paid more than me, simply because he had a higher hourly rate. It made no sense to me.[49]

It is hard to say when charging by the hour was first introduced but the general view is that it was a small New York law firm over 100 years ago. So perhaps it is time for change. Add to that your clients and, probably, your lawyers could do without per hour charging. They do not want to be writing down every six minutes of work that they carry out. Nor do they want to be falling out with their clients at the end of every matter. And if they do not fall out with their clients they will fall out with the finance team or director who will be pushing to charge every minute on the clock. They have worked all hours for the client. The client is delighted with the service but is then annoyed because of an inevitable fee overrun – and let's be honest, it is probably a result of fee creep by fee earners and not even genuine time. It is hardly conducive to good client relationships. The CEO of a client of mine said: "I don't mind my decorator charging by the hour. He starts at 8am. My wife is at home. He finishes at 4pm. I know exactly what he is doing. But when my lawyer does it, I don't know if he is doing the work, if he is playing golf, if he is in management meetings, whether he is efficient or just slow or whether he is doing someone else's work. So when he comes back and tells me he has done 10 hours more than he intended, and despite his quote he is billing for it, forgive me if I'm sceptical."

Pricing provides such an opportunity for innovation. Perhaps I should rephrase that. Pricing provides such an opportunity for innovation for the brave. Being brave is the key. Being brave enough to change a system that has been around and copied by just about every law firm for 100 years or more but which is despised by clients and will continue to ensure that lawyers are the butt of many jokes for years to come unless it is changed. Yet the brave also see the opportunity because good pricing will help a firm to retain clients for years to come. Many clients have been lost by firms as a result of the animosity of price negotiations. Firms often do not even realise why they have lost valuable clients. Pricing also provides an opportunity to win new clients as a result of the flexibility it offers. But possibly, most importantly, is that it provides the chance to earn larger fees when you are prepared to demonstrate value to a client. Something that I have seen few law firms achieve. Pricing is both an art and, if you read behavioural economics, a science. There many authors who can guide you on confident pricing and I would recommend *Value-Based Pricing: Drive Sales and Boost Your Bottom Line by Creating, Communicating and Capturing Customer Value* by Harry Macdivitt and Mike Wilkinson (McGraw-Hill Professional, 2011) and *Pricing with Confidence: 10 Ways to Stop Leaving Money on the Table* (Wiley & Sons, 2008) by Reed Holden and Mike Burton.

There are really only two forms of pricing which lawyers follow (I am not talking here about things such as portfolio pricing, volume pricing or premium models).

There is the cost-based model where you consider your fixed and variable costs, add on a margin and come up with a fee, and then there is market pricing where you charge what the market will pay. Clients will pay more for a service in London than for the same service in Oldham. Branding is important here because the market will always pay more for what it perceives as a premium product. But value is the most important consideration. This is why certain QCs can charge far more than others and be paid vast amounts of money. There is nothing wrong with this. The beauty of a model such as this and where the integrity lies is in fixing that fee ahead of the work. The client can then choose. It does not matter what size the matter is or what area of law you are operating in. When you look at pricing this way you are responding to what your clients want.

- FDs, CEOs and business owners always want certainty on their fees (so do you when you ask the plumber to give you a quote – you hate it when he tells you he has done more work than he quoted for and wants more money or he found problems he had not anticipated – you probably don't trust him). Giving that quote upfront allows the FD or CEO to go elsewhere should he or she wish. Hopefully, you will have done enough to build the personal relationship. Above all, it is the right thing to do. It has integrity and clarity. Clients are comfortable discussing fees. They spend their days negotiating. One client always says to me: "I like having that difficult conversation with you up front on fees – you are a business and I know that if you negotiate hard with me, you will negotiate hard on my behalf." Do not shirk it. Imagine how much the client will appreciate you for it. He respects you more. It emphasises your authority to him. Be positive: iron fist/velvet glove.

- When you have had that conversation and agreed the engagement letter, your relationship just gets better and better because there is no longer an elephant in the room. No one is wondering when the fee issue is going to get raised. There can be no falling out. If you have got it wrong, you may be able to pick it up at the next stage, or even on further work, but you must stick to your quote at all times. If you are very uncertain when quoting, narrow the stages and use your knowledge and experience, but do not avoid it because it is too difficult.

Differential pricing

Differential pricing is not an issue. If you take a plane to France or a train to Eastbourne there will be lots of different prices for the same service. If you go to Timpson to have your shoes repaired you may be charged different prices at different branches because they operate Upside Down Management and each manager can choose his or her own pricing (there are no price boards).[50] John Timpson says that pricing is down to each shop or kiosk. They exercise all the freedom they need to run their business. That gives you all the freedom you need to win work. It comes down to your capacity and what the market will pay.

"Clients are comfortable discussing fees. They spend their days negotiating. One client always says to me – I like having that difficult conversation with you up front on fees – you are a business and I know that if you negotiate hard with me, you will negotiate hard on my behalf."

Getting your pricing wrong can be catastrophic. Even if you have quoted an hourly rate you will quite likely negotiate the fee at the end of the matter, and based on an hourly rate the hours that you have worked will be your cap. Any negotiations will only reduce your fee. It is easy to see how you can lose many thousands of pounds on one phone call. Over the year it is very easy to lose £30k, £40k or £50k due to bad pricing. Over 10 years that can equate to £500k. An awful lot of money to leave on the table. And all for the want of much greater thought before making those calls. And even more for the want of a better pricing strategy.

Understanding different pricing strategies is key to getting pricing right. Moving away from pricing by the hour which has been the norm for many years is not easy but is ultimately far more rewarding both financially and in developing client relationships. Earlier I said that there are two ways to price. However, there are different methods and approaches to pricing as discussed in detail by Holden and Burton in *Pricing with Confidence: 10 Ways to Stop Leaving Money on the Table* (Wiley & Sons, 2008):

- pricing to cover costs;
- pricing to meet the market;
- pricing to close a deal;
- pricing to gain market share.

There is immeasurable value in a pricing strategy. Without a strategy you will not have the confidence to stick with your approach. And confidence is everything. We once invited a pricing consultant in to do some work with our lawyers. He seemed very expensive and my partner felt that she could negotiate his price down. He spent an hour explaining his value and what it would deliver for the firm. At the end of it my partner began to negotiate his fee as I sat back and sipped a second cappuccino. At the end of her speech, he leaned across very gently and confidently and said, "but that's the fee". A perfect example in confidence from a proficient pricing consultant after he had built his value. We should have known better.

Price competition is a fool's game. We have all reduced prices because a competitor was doing it. We have always thought that we will make it up next time. How many times has that happened? Price competition is a fool's game because any fool can play it.

We also need to talk about value because clients love to talk about value. You should get into the habit of understanding your value to clients and discuss it. That is the basis of business exchange. You provide services to clients so they can build their own value. In return they take a part of the value that you helped them build and return it to you in the form of price. That's the way business is supposed to work. But here is the question – do you understand the value that you provide for your client? If you do not, how can you set prices rationally, much less have confidence in the prices that you set? And, as we will see, confidence is the key. In too many cases price is the only thing that clients can differentiate and so the only thing that we sell. The loss of pricing initiative is the combination of two factors:

- the inability to understand the value of your services; and
- the loss of confidence in your pricing strategy.

Thinking about pricing is very important. Time sheets are irritating to complete but they also make you lazy and inefficient in your work. Pricing properly and confidently can help you to win work; it is important to ensure that you get the correct reward and it is important that the client gets the right value. And that must be the starting point, that is, thinking from the outset about the value that you bring to your client. You cannot have confidence in your pricing until you have confidence in the financial value that your offering creates for clients. Most lawyers are convinced that they cannot get this information, but the reality is that clients are eager to tell you. All it takes is asking the right questions and being willing to listen. And slowly (or quickly if you can) changing your mindset. The more that you do it, the more you will build your confidence in your pricing. The more thought you put into it now the more that you will be able to rely on those same thoughts in every transaction that you undertake.

But let's be very specific. How many times have you heard a lawyer say "we want to provide the best value for our clients"? It is a common statement. Every law firm I have been at spouts the same thing. Every managing partner comes out with the same lingo, which has most likely been given to them by MBAs or consultants who then leave them to work it out. And they are incapable of doing so. As a result, it remains a platitude with no substance, constantly spouted to clients who immediately see through it as an irritating piece of aestheticism.

So, what exactly does it mean? Value can mean different things to different people. Does the firm intend to deliver a lot of client benefits but at prices that are similar to the competition? Or does it mean that the firm will offer everything that everyone else does but at lower prices? Or that it is going to meet client needs and hope that it will get some payment? The problem is that the word 'value' in this context is so general that it has no meaning and everyone leaves it that way. And firms that lack a clear definition of value to the client cannot negotiate effectively. After all, how can you build your pricing confidence around a concept that you yourself cannot define? So, you have to get down to the specifics and what matters most to your client.

When talking about value, the key is to avoid both confusion and talking in platitudes. You should focus on the most important definition of value in business-to-business markets. The result is clarity in the financial benefits that your offerings create for clients. There are all kinds of value but I am referring exclusively to financial value. If you decrease your clients' total costs and/or increase their revenues then you increase their profits. That, in very simple terms, is a very clear definition that everyone understands. That should become the focus of your value offering. The key to unlocking all these benefits lies with your ability to understand how your offerings create financial value for your client. Understanding value comes from a process that should be familiar to everyone – asking the client questions about their business. We are not talking big, complex research projects here. Just simple feet-on-the-ground questions. A research mindset. Any knowledge of the value that you deliver gives you greater control and confidence in your pricing. Once your clients trust you and believe that you are sincere in collecting information for their ultimate benefit, that is, to help them run their business, then they will welcome such conversations. Clients want to talk about their business. Their motivation is clear. Once suppliers understand the business issues, the better able those suppliers will be to craft solutions that are relevant and valuable. It takes good listening and probing skills. It requires shifting your internal view (how you think you perform) to an external view (the performance benefits and values that your clients receive). Only the latter view counts. Finally, the analysis has to be done in the context of your competition. Clients do not think about law firms in a vacuum. It is always in the context of how you will perform compared to your competitors.

If you do not have a pricing strategy, then who is setting your prices? If we are honest, what really motivates us is not only losing business but losing it to a competitor. Not only do we lose but the competitor wins. Clients are clearly aware of this and set competitors against each other. So, who is setting your prices? Clearly, your competitors are.

To reverse this cycle and take back control of pricing, it is important to establish a well-reasoned pricing strategy. Intellectually this is not difficult. A pricing strategy is fairly simple. According to Holden and Burton in *Pricing with Confidence: 10 Ways to Stop Leaving Money on the Table* (Wiley & Sons, 2008) there are only three choices: skim, neutral and penetration. Understanding the right one to choose depends on your place in the market, market conditions, and knowing when to change your strategy. The major plus of a pricing model should be the certainty that you give up front to a client that a quote will not change even if the going gets tough, giving the FD or CEO the ability to plan his or her projects. That model gives a client choice. It has integrity at its heart. A client will accept variability of pricing if he or she has the ability to choose. When you fly Easyjet, it is almost guaranteed that the person sitting next to you will have paid a different price. Their model is predicated on low prices until they get to break even and then charging premiums to boost profits. The same applies to Virgin train services. Your pricing may change depending on your market and your competition but also where you are against your own targets and how much you want the work. Apple's strategy is to charge what the market will pay.

In a skimming strategy, prices are set relatively high compared to mainstream competitors. This strategy will maximise revenues generated from the high-end market. In a neutral pricing strategy, prices are set close to those of your main competitors. This strategy is useful when you want to take the focus off the price. Finally, companies that use a penetration strategy set prices quite low compared with the competition in order to make price a driving factor in the purchase decision.

People often opt for penetration pricing. This may be a correct strategy for a young business but if it is maintained for too long it is damaging. Price cuts are easy for competitors to match. It causes problems for lots of reasons including:

- clients who come to you on price are going to be the first to leave when a lower priced competitor comes along. Price-based competition provides the least best competitive advantage;
- unless you have a clear technological advantage, someone will come along who is better at running their business and with a better operation model; and
- ultimately it will damage the brand and condemn the brand to a low price model – where no one wishes to be.

You should get away from penetrative pricing as soon as you can with new clients as well as to educate existing clients. You should clearly be looking at how to skim or neutral price depending on the factors set out above. In each case your ability to skim or neutral price depends on your ability to demonstrate that your offering provides significantly greater financial benefits than the competition. It comes back to your value as a trusted adviser and whether you have built that value. That is where your focus should be with your existing clients and when winning new ones. Be specific.

An obvious fact is that everyone wants value from their lawyers. The reality is that not everyone will pay for it. Clients think differently about value and vendors or suppliers. Some want great relationships. Some only want to buy at the lowest price. To be successful when quoting you need to recognise these differences and craft the right client approach if you do not want to waste time and leave money on the table. There are four types of clients.

- *Fee-based buyers* – These clients buy exclusively on price. They do not care about value-added enhancements, nor about nice documents or fancy offices.

- *Value buyers* – These clients have recognised the flaws of price-only purchasing and often have sophisticated technical and business process people who regulate the value that alternative suppliers and vendors offer. This is often (but not always) larger corporations who have a long history of working with and supporting suppliers and vendors as long as they are willing to improve the cost-effectiveness of their two organisations.

- *Relationship buyers* – These clients only rely on close relationships with suppliers. Relationship buyers trust that their partners will provide solutions that will enhance their business. They become trusted advisers and are involved in the client's business. We may win work from a price buyer or a value buyer but this is where we should be taking all our valued clients. Unlike consultants or other professionals, a lawyer's role should be for life once you achieve trusted adviser status.

- *Cheeky buyers* – Cheeky buyers love to play the pricing game. They have learned that if they focus on price, they often get suppliers to leave money on the table and still provide high-value features.

Finding out what type of buyer you are dealing with is key. It requires you to ask the right, and often direct, questions.

Clearly, when dealing with fee-based buyers you should strip away all extra features. These buyers do not want them – not even if they are free.

"Treat cheeky buyers like fee-based buyers but when they ask for more value tell them it is not available at that price. It is okay to say 'no'. It is often anathema to lawyers but you are also a business person and it really is acceptable."

Do not provide a Rolls Royce but a good working Mini. These buyers present the biggest challenge when trying to change them into relationship buyers. They have no loyalty; recognise it but do not fight it. Stay on their radar but do not waste time.

Value buyers are those clients who understand value. In fact they will often turn down suppliers who do not offer choices and ranges. You must invest in understanding their business and what they want.

Relationship buyers really want to be taken care of. They often need to connect with senior people and executives on a regular basis. Make yourself important. Important people like to deal with important people. Are you one? Offer everything that you can do for them but most of all focus on the personal relationship. Know their business and their needs backwards. These clients will become loyal over time. In dealing with both value and relationship buyers, trust is vital. Work on it to build it and to deliver quality. Respond quickly to their needs, listen and avoid high-pressure selling tactics – show that you care and that you are reliable. Understand what is important to them.

Cheeky buyers are the hardest because they want it all, and they will try to get it. They are cheeky. They will call your bluff. Do not fold and give away huge amounts. Focus on your product and your quality. Tell them and repeat it often that services are not a commodity. Clients will not tell you that because it is not in their interests to do so. Treat cheeky buyers like fee-based buyers but when they ask for more value tell them it is not available at that price. If they want that product, they have to pay a different price. It is okay to say 'no'. It is often anathema to lawyers but you are also a business person and it really is acceptable. Be open and confident but learn to bluff and get up and walk away. You might enjoy it. You will certainly close deals confidently and profitably.

Peter Thiel, the co-founder of PayPal and the first investor in Facebook writes in his book *Zero to One*: "If your product requires advertising or salespeople to sell it, it's not good enough."[51] I guess most of us are not natural salespeople – we are lawyers, so Peter Thiel's comments are encouraging. It was always thought that extroverts are the best salespeople as they do not shrink from making requests; they are assertive and even pushy. But in the most recent research leading from work done by Adam Grant at Wharton,[52] that was found not to be the case. Grant began by asking 300 sales reps to complete personality assessments. He then tracked their performance by revenues. Introverted sales reps did not perform as well as extroverted ones performing at $120 an hour compared to $125 an hour. But what was confounding was the performance of the ambiverts, that is, those in the middle of the spectrum of testing. These performed at $155 an hour and those smack at the midpoint performed at $208 an hour. Since then, more tests have proven that the best salesmen and women are the ambiverts. Why? The conclusions drawn are that extroverts are often too assertive and zealous, do not listen and do not read the signals. They talk too much and listen too little which dulls their understanding of others' perspectives.

Aren't you pleased to be a lawyer and probably, therefore, a boring extrovert or, as I prefer to think, an exciting listener?

One of the best meetings I had recently was with a consultant who wanted to work with us. He had a notebook and for 90 minutes he threw question after question at me and took extensive notes. What was my reaction? I felt he really cared about our business and was genuinely interested. Every now and again he would throw in a gem to show he knew his stuff or would mention something he could do for us which demonstrated that he had the authority we required and that he was definitely the sort of person we needed: knowledgeable, thoughtful, thorough, well prepared and who wanted to make a difference to our business. But it was brought about through very authoritative questioning. He made me enjoy talking about our business (which is never difficult) and he got across just how much he could help us. He was already demonstrating his value and we had not yet engaged him. The point is that you can demonstrate value at every touchpoint and with every communication.

So here are some final thoughts on pricing as you look to innovate and determine a pricing strategy. Getting pricing right is a key part of your product. Giving and communicating value to your client should be paramount. Giving them certainty should be critical before they embark on working with you. Getting fair remuneration for your work is key for you.

You must see pricing as an opportunity to engage your clients in discussion and encourage them to see the value that you are providing. It will build and strengthen your relationship with your client, not weaken it, so relish the discussions. Be confident, bold and upfront. There are so many opportunities to be innovative when developing pricing strategies.

The stages of pricing

- Engage your client in open and wide-ranging discussion about the project for which they wish to engage you. Take your time, show interest and ask lots of questions (keep a note in one of your folders of a long list of possible questions until you are totally comfortable with this). Think laterally. Think of the effect of your project on the wider business, demonstrate your commerciality by displaying your understanding of the business and the markets, take lots of notes and stop talking in order to write down important points to show emphasis and understanding; show that you both care and empathise. Continue to build a rapport. Tell the client that you need to understand everything because you want to produce a contract that you would be happy for your granny to sign or a settlement that you would recommend to your granny. Do some initial work for free as a gesture. Draw them in so they would not dream of going anywhere else. Be that trusted adviser that they want and that you want to be. If you are confident and looking for a relationship, perhaps ask them to set the fee for the first job.

- Do not give a quote on the spot. Tell them you will think it through and will send them a note with your thoughts. Explain that you want to get the price right so that you do not have to discuss it again and you can focus fully on the job in hand and on being part of the team. They have a job to be done and you believe that you can do it for them better than anyone else: "So let's get a fee that we are both happy with, agreed and out of the way, so we can focus on what needs to be done." Now is your opportunity to build value. Talk to others if you need help on pricing and the issues involved. Then put together and send them a comprehensive note. Quote back to them lots of things that they have told you about the business to let them know that you have listened. Use language which is familiar to them. Set out why the project is important and put it into context in the business, for example, why they are choosing to part company with the CEO – the business has come as far as it can and needs to move up a gear and this is the first step in doing that – it needs to be done quickly, efficiently and cost-effectively (if that is what they are asking for) etc. Set out in detail everything that you will do and the benefit it will be to them and list each piece of work. Unless you tell them they will not know what you will be doing. Explain clearly why and how they will benefit. Set out your price as part of how you work, that is, tell them things they want to hear including how you will make their job easier. Your aim is to get the best settlement or agreement. Tell them you will focus on the important issues that affect the business, you will focus on issues and not personalities, you will provide them with status reports or updates, you will give them a report prior to board meetings, you will write internal memos for them, etc; tell them whatever you have learned from them in your discussions that they would appreciate. Focus on your behaviours and then add: "As part of that we believe it is very important that you and your finance people are able to have certainty over the price that this will cost you. The fee is £xxx (do not give a round number as if you have plucked it out of the air). This will not change. [Then assume it is agreed.] It is important that we get things underway as quickly as we can. I have changed my diary in order that I can be at your office tomorrow morning to take instructions. Does that suit?"

- Once the fee is agreed, step back and work out how you can make your procedures as efficient as possible. How can you reduce the number of meetings? How can you ensure that all negotiations are done in one go? How can you use Skype? How can you manage the other lawyers? The more efficient you are, the more money you will make and the happier the client will be. Remember, the best referees are hardly noticed in a good football match. Your client wants to stay focused on the business and you can help him or her to do that.

If the client challenges your price, do not fold and agree to what he or she suggests. That shows a lack of integrity in your pricing and your client will immediately recognise that. There is no way back. If he or she suggests that someone else is cheaper, do not give up; ask if he or she can explain what is on offer. They are likely to be comparing apples with pears. When they have explained to you it is likely that there is not as much detail in the competing offer as you have given – and the devil is in the detail. Explain that you really want to do the job and want to form the relationship. Ask for a little more time to reflect. Use this time to refine your offering, perhaps taking some things out that they haven't valued. If you cannot find a way to do this and you want the job, go back and explain that you will do it at the competitor's price because you want to show your quality and build a long-lasting relationship that will work for both of you. If you make concessions, ask for something in return; for example, at the end of the matter if they like what you have done ask if they will introduce you to one potential new client at a lunch. That will really cement your relationship. Best of all, go and see them at their office and explain the above.

This would be a bold innovation for you to adopt but the rewards for clients and your firm are immense. Of course, it requires trust in your people and that requires education and the removal of certain comfort blankets such as time sheets. But the plus side is if you get it right you will have happier clients, happier lawyers and, if you really get it right, larger revenues. The real key to a good pricing strategy is value, communication of value and confidence. Many law firm leaders believe that that leaves too much to trust which is a shame.

Designing lives

Law firm management teams are in an unbelievable position. They have so much control over the lives of so many. It is an awesome responsibility. Their decisions affect the lives of not only the lawyers and everyone who works for the firm but also those closest to them, their family and friends. Many stories abound in the industry of divorces due to the demands of the job, lost relationships with children and parents because of long hours and inefficient processes, and lack of authority and leadership from partners. It is sad that the industry is now known for the 'beasting' of young lawyers rather than for nurturing and creating better citizens. 'Beasting' is a term which originated in London and refers to the overworking of young lawyers in (generally) large commercial law firms. Lawyers will often be in the office doing very little during the day but then because of process and partner inefficiencies will be expected to stay all night. The sad fact is that it is perpetual, and when the once-young lawyers become partners they treat the next generation of young lawyers the same way.

So, the opportunity to innovate is immense – society is changing and law firms have the opportunity to change and to be different. But practices are so entrenched that it will take brave leadership and caring people. Too many law firms pay lip service to caring for their people. Pretending to care and pretending to innovate. One young lawyer recently said to me "my firm has a working from home policy. It is called after nine and at weekends". And one senior partner of a Magic Circle firm told me "if they can't stand the heat they should get out of the kitchen".

But life has moved on and dinosaurs such as that Magic Circle partner are not relevant in the new world. Law firms are already losing some of their best talent. It began with women who wanted to give priority to the raising of children but it is now lawyers of both genders who realise that they can design their lives themselves as well as earn more money in the new style law firms such as gunner*cooke*.

Time is now of the essence and there is little of it left as these firms will begin to take their best lawyers. Who would want to be in an organisation that designs your life for you, that tells you when you can work and often even when you can sleep? Or that tells you how many hours you must work a day, how many hours of business development you must do and how many hours of *pro bono* you must complete? I appreciate that it is not long since slavery was abolished but law firms continue to act as if they own people just because they pay them.

We are about to begin a major transition that is even more life-changing than new technology and is causing an increase in longevity. People born today will mostly live to be 100. Some will live to be 125 and I recently read that some scientists are predicting that there will be people who will live to be 1,000. This is because of the eradication of diseases. A long life could be a great gift but not, I guess, if you are tied to the way many of our traditional law firms operate. Lynda Gratton and Andrew Scott in their book, *The 100-Year Life*,[53] write that a child born in the West today has a more than 50% chance of living to be 105, while by contrast a child born over a century ago had a less than 1% chance of living to that age. Over the last 200 years life expectancy has expanded at a steady rate of more than two years every decade. This means that if you are now 20 you have a 50% chance of living to more than 100, if you are 40 you have an even chance of living to 95, and if you are 60 then you have a 50% chance of making it to 90 or more.

This lengthening of life is a crucial debate. No longer will people work in the traditional way – 50 years, a clock and retire. They will need to work longer to pay for their lengthening life and they will seek greater happiness in their work. People will set their goals differently and already we can see that the millennials are not as insecure about finances as we and our parents are. They are greater seekers of happiness, of experiences and of altruism.

The evidence of wellbeing and happiness is growing fast and has attracted the interests of numerous studies and government funding around the world. The UK government regularly collects UK data.

The Dalai Lama once said that "the very purpose of life is to be happy". You may have observed that, these days, there are more and more books on ways to be happy. There is the Danish way of being happy – the Danes are supposedly the happiest people in the world – and then there is the Swedish way and even the South Korean way (big on measuring happiness); and the most recent book I saw was about the Japanese way. Ever since former Prime Minister, David Cameron, announced that measuring our happiness was just as important, if not more important than measuring GDP, there have been numerous studies on happiness by government organisations, educational facilities and NGOs. In every study concerning what we can do about our happiness and contentment the same five ways of improving our circumstances come to the top – consistently so – and so we would be foolish to ignore the findings.

First is the importance of our social relationships. People who see others regularly or who belong to a meaningful group are likely to experience higher levels of happiness. Another is the importance of mindfulness or curiosity – at its simplest this is noticing things around you and appreciating and being grateful for everything. Another feel-good factor involves giving. Individuals are at their happiest when given the opportunity to help or spend money on others – we now pay bonuses in two halves, one for the person and the other to help our people think of giving to others. Another route to happiness is learning. Studies show that learning something new, particularly in later life, has a positive impact on our lives, and raises our self-esteem and confidence. And finally, studies show a consistent corollary between health and happiness. The higher your own health and fitness is, the higher your own levels of satisfaction.

The statistics show that when you have a happier workforce you will retain them longer, they will win more and retain more clients for you and they will help you to attract better quality people. And your revenues

"*People who see others regularly or who belong to a meaningful group are likely to experience higher levels of happiness.*"

and your profitability will improve. And I guess you can add to that that you and the leadership will feel more virtuous and happier for the changes you have made.

So where do you start to innovate? You might try asking your people what they think. The Measuring Stick is a useful HR tool found online that will help you to gauge the happiness of your people. But do not be satisfied with the results and do not take things too literally. As I wrote earlier, listen – but also be prepared to lead and to do the right thing, and instinctively know what the right thing is.

That is why you are a leader – you believe in the lives of your people. If you believe in their happiness and their families' happiness then create a project group that cares and give the team the bold and challenging remit of beginning the process of building better lives. This is one project where just the fact that you are doing it will raise the morale of the firm. Invite anyone who can contribute to come and talk to the team, seek out executives from other businesses where they put people before profit and make contact with consultants with experience of new-style businesses. Trial ideas constantly in focused groups. If you want to trial a five-hour working day then try it first in one part of the business and measure its success against what is important, not just to the individuals but also to the firm. Begin a change in culture and educate everyone on the change needed. This group is one that should never actually come to an end because there will always be something to improve upon. But only if you value your people.

Training young lawyers

One area above many others that is crying out for innovation is the training of young lawyers. Much of this goes back to the initial training that lawyers undertake at university. I cannot recall one subject that I learned at university which became valuable when I went into practice. In fact, quite the opposite. I studied lots of social and welfare subjects at university because I was idealistic and wanted to improve the world. I still do. But the reality is I became a corporate lawyer. Not once did I feel that my lack of corporate education held me back. It is a miracle that our education system is held in such high regard internationally and in my view is probably a result of history and one or two exceptional institutions. The system is still grounded in agricultural needs and little innovation has been introduced in the last 100 years. Michael Gove, the former Secretary of State for Education, claimed that the most important element in the quality of education was the teacher.[54] We have terrific people entering the academic world all the time, many after years in industry, and yet we limit them in their ability to do what they know is right from primary level through to the final education tier. We need people in education who are true entrepreneurs and innovators. Our universities fail to deliver and prepare our lawyers for the future. It is bizarre that a lawyer can first do a degree in zoology, or any other subject that he or she wishes, and then do a 12-month conversion course and is seen as no different from a student who has studied law for three years. Quite an indictment on law studies.

The very first innovation should be stronger partnerships between law firms and universities designing courses and methods of working that will deliver better-educated and passionate lawyers. Universities have access to the best three years of a future lawyer's life so they should not waste a minute of it. Not only should they teach the core subjects and more specialised academic subjects but they should also address other personal and professional skills that lawyers will require such as business development or understanding balance sheets, or social skills such as resilience, or skills that will make them better citizens. And they should provide much greater practical and vocational work. I cannot help but think it is an opportunity lost. Three years of dedicated opportunity to help convert our future lawyers into wonderful people. Universities appear to be too much an extension of school. But during this time the preparation should be more focused on the years ahead, showing future lawyers the wonderful profession they have chosen and igniting their passion to be the best that they can be.

The failure of our universities coupled with the oversupply of lawyers and lack of jobs when they emerge provides an opportunity for some of our larger law firms to partner with a university to design courses to deliver the next generation of lawyer – the aim being to prepare them better than previous generations.

But learning does not begin and end at university and law firms can and should see themselves as learning organisations; businesses where self-improvement becomes a key part of the culture. Lawyers often choose to be lawyers because they enjoy learning, perhaps more so than young people who choose other disciplines or future paths. An organisation that employs this nature for the improvement of the lawyer and so the improvement of the firm will be maximising a key opportunity. When a lawyer leaves a firm he or she should leave as a better lawyer and a better person, and should leave the firm and the role better than it was when he or she arrived.

Putting much more effort into training our young lawyers by building a learning culture, setting learning goals and producing collaborative learning plans will not only produce better lawyers but it will provide future leadership for the firm and will encourage future innovators. Organisations do not succeed by staying the same. They are people businesses and so investing in the future is, well, *res ipsa loquitur* – I love that phrase. When Blockbuster went out of business, like several other iconic businesses over the last few years, the onset of Netflix or other competitors was often blamed. The reality is that they put themselves out of business by not keeping up with the changes that ultimately destroyed them.

Becoming a learning organisation will help your firm to recruit the best lawyers and will also give you the advantage of making your lawyers the best at everything they do. Of 12 industrials that formed the original Dow Jones index, GE is the only one that remains part of that index. The company's success is attributed to Jack Welch who during his tenure grew it to be the largest firm in the world. Welch transformed GE into a learning organisation. During his tenure GE's value increased by 4,000%.

A lot of learning currently undertaken in law firms is formal learning.

It is intended to meet specific needs and new tasks. Education differs in that it is more long term and not so focused on immediate needs. Large multinationals begin to prepare future CEOs to run their divisions or subsidiary businesses from the outset. Law firms dismiss the power of leadership training believing that it is perfectly possible for a managing partner to be a litigator on a Friday evening and running a multi-million pound business on Monday morning – the enlightened ones sending them on a three-month crash course at Harvard.

But a learning organisation is much more than a sophisticated training programme. It is imbued in the culture and draws on best practice from every part of the business. It is top down and is a way of working and existing. It is the way in which lessons are learned across the business, how information is shared and how the office is organised. It is how the leadership talks. It is the revering of educators and the wise use of coaches and mentors. It is how lawyers progress. It is creating a giving culture where those anxious to give are rewarded properly. It is about listening to the organisation. It is about listening to those outside and from more enlightened industries. It is about creating transparency with the leaders openly talking and promoting and being proud of the learning culture. It is about not confining the learning and education to creating better lawyers and about creating more balanced people and better citizens. It is about not worrying if they leave your business but being proud of their future achievements. It is about encouraging questions and challenging and eliminating insecurities. It is about encouraging failure as part of the learning process – there is no such thing as failure, the only failure is not trying.

But building such an organisation does not just happen, it requires desire and it requires design and it requires passion and it requires leadership.

Most lawyers begin with the premise that clients must always come first and training or education is indispensable. So it will be no easy task to change that culture of thought.

There should be no restriction on the extent of the training of our

"One of the first challenges of the leaders of the law firm is to find role models. Lawyers have been taught a certain way and pass that on. They are also often quite insecure."

young lawyers. Most law firms seem to think that only senior lawyers should be allowed to develop business. I will always remember the head of business development, a tough, no-nonsense individual brought in from the banks who used to say: "We send our young men and women to fight on the front line at 18, I can't see why they can't go and talk to businesses."

One of the first challenges of the leaders of the law firm is to find role models. Lawyers have been taught a certain way and pass that on. They are also often quite insecure. They are insecure about others being better than them and insecure about others who are better than them taking their clients. As a leader you must set an example and your project team must include the already existing role models that you can find in the business. Any insecure partner will hold the project back.

Start by asking questions of your group.

- Do we have a learning culture?
- Do we have a culture of self-improvement?
- Do we challenge ourselves to continuously improve things?
- Do we show our people that it is okay to fail?
- Do we take views from our people?
- Do we encourage our lawyers to speak their minds?
- Do our partners see themselves as coaches or mentors – all of them?
- Do we respect each other's views?
- Do we have big enough budgets for our education programmes?
- Do our employees like their jobs? Do we ask them?
- Do people help each other?
- Do people give credit where it is due?
- Would learning programmes help our recruitment?
- How diverse are our learning programmes?
- Do we teach soft skills well enough, for example, business development, running meetings, client care etc?
- Do we look at our people holistically?
- What is the essence of our programmes? Is it to make them better people?

- What is the attendance rate at our programmes?
- What excuses do lawyers make for not being there?
- Can we learn from other organisations?

Moving a culture to a learning culture will not be easy for any managing partner particularly when he or she is judged by the short-term goal of profits per partner. But it is the right thing to do not only for the young lawyers but also for the long-term success of the firm. How do you want to be remembered?

To help your thinking in this area I would encourage you to read *Building an Innovative Learning Organisation* by Russell Sarder.[55]

Modern marketing

I cannot claim to be an expert in marketing but what I do know is that marketing cannot be left to the marketing team. It should be a combination of the leadership and the marketing department. It is a partnership where one cannot work without the other. The marketing team is, and should be, expected to market the brand. The brand needs to be designed. Few law firms design their brand leaving it to happenstance. A firm's brand is an extension of its culture which takes us back to the early chapters of this book. A marketing team cannot be left to work in isolation. A managing partner who has been thrust into the role will often find it easier to stay aloof from marketing and leave it to his 'professional' colleague. That would be a mistake.

Another mistake that leaders often make, again because they do not feel comfortable, is bringing in consultants who will spend many hours and lots of money undertaking surveys only to tell you what you already know. A brand can and should be aspirational and if you are not where you want to take the business by all means organise a focus group of some of your key clients who are loyal to your business and who will tell you the truth. But the leader must lead the group and must take on the job of listening to others and developing the aspiration for your brand. It should be a key part of your vision.

Marketing is a key function in the business. Its role is that of persuading others (employees or existing clients) to become fans and ambassadors or it can be aimed at new clients. What the leader and the marketing team and your salespeople/lawyers have in common is the need to persuade people. Daniel Pink has written a book called *To Sell is Human*[56] because, as he says at the outset, you are selling every day whether you are asking your children to mow the lawn or your wife or husband to cook dinner or your client to instruct you.

Your marketing team should be the best persuaders in the business but they must be closely aligned in working with the leadership team as they design the brand.

Marketing in law firms has long been very basic and less than thoughtful, and a lot of it is clearly irrelevant to the client. This comes through in the marketing material sent to clients announcing the latest deal which boasts about the number of offices or the firm's position in the league tables. It is archaic and, frankly, embarrassing.

Marketing is no longer about you at all. It is completely about the client. The only way for marketing to engage and therefore ultimately be successful is to provide value to the customer in their specific situation. Bombarding them with tombstones of transactions that you have been involved in will only irritate them in this busy new world. Shouting at them in this way no longer works.

The result is that marketing is no longer a means to an end. It is an end and an experience in itself. It should be an experience by providing value to the business in which it chooses to interact. It is an experience, product or service in its own right.

Of course, to achieve the above will require an IT investment that will give you greater knowledge about your client databases and allow your clients to access your marketing at their time of choosing. A good CRM system and an analytics web service is essential.

Innovation in this area will mean that your marketing team is likely to look at itself totally differently. Clients are no longer pawns to be marketed to for the sole purpose of generating transactions or to be sent snippets of information about things that you have done. A firm's success is no longer about telling them how good you are, no matter how creative your campaign is. Members of the public at large are now great influencers in your marketing. Previously you were able to control messaging, but now the best that you can do is facilitate it. We used to say that the customer is king but now the customer is your partner and your ambassador, and they have an increasing influence over how others view you. Their view of you is instant. Conversations are happening online all the time. You want to be part of that conversation, and you want your clients to be too, but you also want to encourage positive conversation about you. Everyone is a marketeer these days so part of the role of the marketing team is to direct conversations about your firm that are positive – like the Nordstrom stories.

Marketing is an end in itself and your innovation discussions should include the value that your marketing can create for your clients. Marketing today is about client attention. Persuade clients to engage in conversations and provide them with value and they will give more freely of their time. Value is created around the services that you provide. Merely concentrating on the product is not enough. Unlike in the traditional funnel method of marketing, the new model of marketing is totally inclusive and subject to data protection rules so you no longer need to rule numbers of clients out of marketing information. You do not need to exclude anyone because they can contribute to the conversation and their word-of-mouth recommendations can contribute to helping you to be noticed. At the same time, you need to understand where they are active, for example, industry blogs, social network forums, events etc.

Marketing is one of many areas that has changed, and is continuing to change rapidly, and where more and more innovative approaches are required.

Business development

Winning new clients is the oxygen of every practice and yet law firms have a very elitist approach to rainmaking. A sales and service culture should be embedded in every organisation. Sadly, lawyers often believe that sales is beneath them and are critical of client-winning partners who they prefer to see as academically less gifted than others, and this is reflected in how they are treated and remunerated, often preferring to reward on the number of hours billed than the source of the client. Changing and promoting a sales or business development culture is key to an organisation and is clearly open to innovation. A simple assessment of your firm's fees will show that a substantial proportion will have been sourced by just a few partners.

An innovation team needs to focus primarily on the change of culture and on building the internal reputation of rainmakers in the organisation so that young lawyers in particular see the benefit of rainmaking. At the same time, opportunities should be given to these rainmakers to pass on their secrets and their stories. You will be surprised and they will take it for granted because it is second nature to them. If you want to create a business development culture, the stories and the legends that surround them have to be told time and time again.

Below are a few guidelines to help to understand the secrets of rainmakers and encourage a business development culture.

If developing business is important to a partner then he or she must give it the priority that it requires – above everything (and I really mean everything) else.

I recall an interview by Terry Wogan (this dates me). He was interviewing a world-renowned violinist – so renowned I have forgotten her name. He asked her why she was such a late developer compared with the youth of violinists these days. Her reply was a great lesson for all of us. She said that in her early career she would do everything else before she did her practice – the housework, the shopping, meet with her agent, etc. It was only when she realised that practice was her priority and the most important part of her career, and came before anything else, that her career started to take off.

What a great lesson. Most lawyers will tell you that their work/clients come first. Hard to argue but actually it is not difficult to fit in one hour of business development before the day begins. Lawyers will argue that sometimes they need to attend meetings first thing or write long emails or make umpteen phone calls. I would argue that they are most definitely wrong. Organising your diary each day to enable you to spend the first hour talking to potential clients, emailing them, or setting up meetings or visits is far more important. The rest can fit in following this first hour. If the firm reinforces just how important this is it will quickly become habit-forming and part of the culture. Priority should be to build for the future, to deliver on a plan. Self-discipline and prioritising business development will make all the difference to the top line of a business. If you create and promote this culture it will quickly become second nature and will revolutionise the business.

Rainmaking is tough. Academic lawyers rarely understand what is involved in winning major clients and just how personal it is. I recall taking a client out for lunch with another partner. On return, he said: "Now we've done that, let's hope the work comes in." How naive and wrong could he be? I talked recently to a friend who described how he met his wife: "We met at 7pm and talked until about 10pm. I felt good. We met again a few days later. We met at 7pm again and by midnight I knew that she was 'the one'. We'd talked about life, values, her politics, her passions, the past and the future and I was filled with an excitement that I hadn't felt before. As clichéd as it sounds, I was sure I would end up marrying this woman."

It is interesting how this story matches so many others. That sense of knowing sets in around the first few dates for many people. It is also interesting how so many people make big decisions in a big way in a business context. People often think that winning a client takes a one-hour meeting or a lunch, but any good rainmaker will tell you it takes lots more than that and the danger is that you close off too quickly – before you have done your 'eight hours' – rather than work out what the next hour should look like.

Big purchasing decisions will take about eight hours, whether you are buying a new car, making a career move or engaging a consultant. When you add up all the time spent on making these decisions you can be fairly sure it will amount to around eight hours.

It is also logical that if someone is willing to invest eight hours getting to know you or about a topic, it is because they are interested. If they had not felt any connection, they would not have hit the eight-hour mark. They would have walked away. During those eight hours, people establish their criteria, look for need, develop an emotional connection, build trust, rapport and understanding. Then something happens at the eight-hour mark – you get sick of thinking about it and you are ready to make a decision.

Do not ignore the eight-hour rule – do not force the deal too early. But when it is time to close – then close – do not miss your opportunity.

Japanese businessmen do this. They will rarely talk business until after a round or two of golf. It can actually blow the deal to bring up business too soon.

None of this matters if you are selling on price or selling something trivial but if you are seeking to win a major new client or build a new relationship the eight-hour rule is paramount. But whether it is seven, or ten, or three or four hours, the fact is that it takes time.

To scale this concept, your goal is to clock up eight hours with as many people as possible. Not in a creepy, annoying way but you do want people to want to spend eight hours with you. Maybe you host great parties, or chair great industry meetings or play great golf, or just take people out for coffee once a month. As long as people like spending time with you, it will not be wasted.

Two great things then happen after the eight-hour relationship:
- you don't feel uneasy offering something of value; and
- you are more confident of the answer you will get.

Peter Thiel, co-founder of PayPal and Palantir, says sales work best when hidden.[57] This explains why almost everyone whose job involves distribution – whether in sales, marketing or advertising – has a job title that has nothing to do with those things. People who sell advertising are called 'account executives', people who sell customers work in 'business development', people who sell companies are 'investment bankers' and people who sell themselves are called 'politicians'.

Whatever the career, sales ability distinguishes superstars from the others. In other cultures it is held up as role model behaviour. On Wall Street, a new hire starts as an analyst wielding technical expertise, but his or her goal is to become a dealmaker. A lawyer prides himself on professional credentials but law firms are led by the rainmakers who bring in big clients. The most successful actors or musicians are often the best salespeople in a crowded market.

It is that important. The most fundamental reason that even business people underestimate the importance of sales is the systematic effort to hide it at every level of every field in a world secretly driven by it.

Sales is an art, but it is a complicated art, driven by people's needs, driven by psychology, responded to by emotional intelligence, and powered by discipline and prioritising. Successful lawyers, musicians, people from every profession understand that and spend hours and hours learning the art and then selling their skills. So, if you want to create a business development culture make sure the most important hour of the day – the first hour – is given over to reading about selling, practising and actioning selling projects, following through on everything and learning the gentle art of quiet persistence – and never letting go. Show desire, faith, planning and persistence – that is what it takes.

There is often a lack of education surrounding sales. Most lawyers believe it to be about being at the beck-and-call of a client, being totally available and jumping to their tune. This is a misconception and no one would have any respect for a lawyer like that. You would never get through the prism to become a trusted and then a personal adviser to a client if that is how you behave.

Jean-Pierre Villiers (JP) is one of London's most highly paid fitness trainers.[58] He does not need everyone to be a client, he only needs a select number of people who want a dedicated level of service that most trainers are too busy to deliver.

When he started out he charged £45 per hour and was burned out from working long hours. He then met Daniel Priestley, a successful entrepreneur, who taught him a different way to operate. At first he resisted but as he believed more, he trusted more.

He worked hard to find his niche. He wrote a book, tailored his offering and worked on raising his profile. He spoke at business events and appeared in exclusive magazines. He positioned himself as a key person of influence in the eyes of an elite target audience. He began to build a new market around him – the JP market.

He thought differently, found his niche and focused. Food for thought. It takes confidence and lots of thinking in order to separate yourself. But it is worth every bit of effort.

The Paris department store, Galeries Lafayette, is one of the world's most famous places for high-end fashion and accessories. Inside is an exclusive area for designer handbags but customers cannot enter just by walking in, they have to queue up at the entrance. An attendant comes by and asks what you will be looking at in the store. The wait is not normally too long – only about 10 minutes or so and the attendants are quite pleasant (you may have experienced the same at Abercrombie & Fitch in London). Then you are in the store and you can browse designer handbags. You buy something you want – you do not take too long because you are conscious of the queues outside. You pay an arm and a leg. The store attendants thank you and you leave feeling good.

A couple of streets away is a store full of handbags, belts, shoes and jewellery. A man shouts in French and English how his stock is on sale, it's cheap and half-price. People try to ignore him, look the other way. The store is almost empty.

The handbags in both these stores are not that different. Clearly, the designer bags cost a little more and last a little longer than the cheaper ones, but the uninitiated may struggle to see which ones are better.

There is of course one big difference – the price. The brand name bags are 50 times more expensive yet they are what people queue for.

The reason is people do not buy what others want to sell. They buy what other people want to buy. We buy properties and clothes that other people want. We buy from consulting firms that others use and we invest in companies that others are throwing money at. Yet countless people go to great lengths to show how badly they want to sell something. They scream into the streets that they have cheap products to sell.

Service providers take on clients without setting any boundaries. They answer calls late at night, get paid late and incur costs. Everything says, "I will do anything for a sale". The more people and companies do that the more they turn people off. The more a potential buyer sees you are desperate to sell something the more they wonder why you are desperate. Your goal is to place a high value on what you do and work with people of like mind. Set your boundaries, have your terms and protect your space so you can deliver something special. The skill comes in making something available without forcing it on people. Your job is to celebrate the people who are already buying from you and hold them in the highest esteem. Take care to ensure they feel good about what they have bought and give them more than they expected. Do not rush off, build the relationship. When they feel good about buying from you, they will tell people they bought from you. When they tell people, others will want to buy. It is not about price – it is about personal branding.

I have recently returned from a few days' cycling in the Champagne country (did you know there are 15,000 champagne houses in France – quite a holiday). I went with a friend, who has just stepped down as FD of a £2.5 billion business and who is a constant buyer of professional services. He said he has never failed to get the provider he wanted because of price. If the one he wanted was the most expensive he would negotiate them down on price and perhaps limit the scope in order get the person he wanted (though, as he said, he may tell the others that they lost on price – easy way out). So there you have it. Makes sense doesn't it? Buyers want to work with their favoured provider – price is just a negotiation point. It is all about your brand.

Rainmaking is an art. It is personal and it is about creating a personal brand through motivation and self-discipline. Innovation should be

"Service providers take on clients without setting any boundaries. They answer calls late at night, get paid late and incur costs. Everything says, 'I will do anything for a sale'. The more people and companies do that the more they turn people off."

focused on creating a culture to profile and make role models of your natural rainmakers so let them be part of changing the culture – let them explain what they do.

Creating a rainmaking culture means that everyone in your business can be encouraged to grow your business but, of course, that may not be the right course for you. Some law firms are now establishing sales teams. The premise is that lawyers advise on the law, managers manage and salespeople sell. This is a much more professional approach considering sales strategies, account plans, playbooks and methodologies.

Of course, there is room for both but the important thing is to see business development as a key area of your innovation programme.

Managing technology

Richard and Daniel Susskind wrote in their book *The Future of The Professions*:

> *In Tomorrow's Lawyers we predict that the legal world will change "more radically over the next two decades" than "over the last century". Numerous commentators have echoed this view of a legal profession on the brink of unprecedented upheaval. In truth, the working practices of lawyers and judges have not changed much since the time of Charles Dickens.*[59]

There is no doubt that much change is coming. And it is coming so quickly that it will be difficult to keep up. Bill Gates said: "Information technology and business are becoming inextricably interwoven. I don't think anybody can talk meaningfully about one without talking about the other."[60]

The Susskinds explain that adults now spend more than two hours a day online and Google processes more than one billion search queries every day. Just writing about these facts will make this book soon seem dated because of the speed of change. It has been predicted that 28 billion devices ranging from wearable devices to vehicles will be connected to the Internet by 2020. Technology is changing the way we live, work, train, communicate, travel and how we transfer information, and it is changing so fast that it is impossible to keep up. Much of it is good but not always. It will help you to compete but there may be a cost to that and a cost to your people. So you need to fully understand where technology can help, where you need to incorporate it into everyday life, where you should outsource to experts and where you should invest.

It is essential that you involve experts but it is even more important that you understand your business and its needs. A long time ago, and long before the digital and online explosion, I worked in the legal department of a major multinational corporation. I recall the FD saying: "When the IT team ask for a million pounds who am I to argue, it's like a black hole." So this problem is not new. For years we have believed that IT is the panacea to all problems. We have been bamboozled by IT salespeople convincing us just what we need and because we are ignorant or do not wish to show our ignorance we have not challenged them. We have been convinced by customer relationship management systems and have been told that they are the answer to our marketing woes. Yet, I have not met one IT manager who has been able to tell me that their IT system is more than 50% utilised, and that is because it is dependent on both human input and, more importantly, human motivation. That is not the responsibility of the system.

Vast sums of money are wasted on technology so one part of your innovation programme should be to ensure that your money is well spent in this uncertain area by asking questions such as:

- Do we have to buy?
- Can we outsource?
- Do we need the latest version?
- Is it tried and tested?

Innovation should be about being client obsessed and digitally enabled, not the other way around. Technology is important, of course, but client obsession should drive all your discussions and all your decisions. What problem are we solving? Innovation is about solving clients' needs so ensure that you have a client-facing partner working with your IT department before you make costly decisions. The client should be at the leading edge, not the technology.

Leadership

The partnership vehicle was originally created to allow no more than 20 people to be in business together and to share profit among themselves. Clearly, management and leadership structures were a lot easier when fewer than 20 partners were able to congregate around a table to discuss the key decisions rather than partnerships which can now be numbered in the hundreds or even thousands. But whether the firm has 10 partners or 1,000 partners, leadership is key. Large corporate organisations understand the value of leadership training and will educate and train potential leaders from an early age and ensure that they gain experience in focused areas. Leadership is an art.

It should be noted that the appointment of managing partners can be political and akin to leading government or a political party with manifestos, debates and campaigns. This is the result of personal ambition and goes against the integrity that great leaders – 'servant leaders' who will always put their organisation first – demonstrate. It is often the most successful rainmaker or the lawyer with the best clients who seeks this role or who is encouraged to stand for it. Does that make them the best leader or the best visionary? Personal ambition is not a reliable characteristic of good leadership. More likely it is the opposite.

Leadership sets the vision, determines the goals and forms the culture of a business. As we have seen, leadership is key to innovation and change. Many of the skills of leadership such as passion and determination are intrinsic to a character of an individual but many skills are learned in the same way that anything else is learned, through education, whether that be practical, or in a schoolroom, or by self-learning. CEOs not only have to deal with day-to-day operations but they must have the skills to address key areas such as competition, sales, marketing, people management, innovation, service and leadership.

It could easily be argued that it is arrogant of law firms to believe that the CEO or managing partner needs to be a lawyer because only a lawyer can understand the legal business. In fact, a law firm is one of the simplest businesses there is. It does not require any special skills to understand it but it does require special skills to be a CEO or managing partner. To be a litigator or corporate lawyer on a Friday evening and then be expected to run the business on a Monday morning is simply not credible. The law must innovate. Over the last 30 years or so more and more specialisms have developed within law firms. Banking broke away from corporate and now there are many different strands of finance. Tax broke away and there are many different specialities of tax. So why do lawyers operate under the misapprehension that running the business is not a specialist role and could be undertaken by any of them? In that time business school courses have burgeoned and it is hard to imagine how a CEO of a sizeable operation would take on the role without a decent MBA. Business training and education are key to the running of any respectable organisation. Until such time as a law firm has invested heavily in management training for its younger lawyers and developed them into future leaders, a law firm should look outside for professional management.

At the same time, the boards of law firms are often populated by practising lawyers, often voted in by their partners and who are seen not as leaders but as there to represent their interests. Very rarely are non-executive directors from the business world invited to join the boards of law firms. This hampers the sort of good business debate that is required in order to move law firms forward, to innovate and to address key business issues in a well-informed way.

What is important about leadership is the ability and the courage to lead. Because of the nature of legal partnerships many managing partners spend their time writing long papers and convincing partners of the route forward because they need their vote. Managing partners need to develop the authority of leadership and partners must let them lead. Reforming the leadership structure and how the leadership team leads is a key part of that. If a managing partner is working with a good executive and professional management committee then he or she needs a good and diverse board to help devise the correct strategies for the firm going forward. The board should be steered away from operational matters and meet less frequently but their meetings should be more strategic, visionary and efficient.

This is possibly the hardest area of innovation for a managing partner because the likely result may be to ultimately replace himself or herself. So it requires a selfless managing partner who can look beyond his or her tenure to bring in professional management and leadership to take the business forward.

Chapter 8
Accountability

A body of men holding themselves accountable to nobody ought not to be trusted by anybody.
Thomas Paine

John's story
John exited his drive at his usual time and switched on Radio 4. More Brexit. He rummaged in his glove compartment as he merged onto a major road and found a CD of David Austin Grey and put it in the CD player. He was delighted at the first couple of meetings of the Imagineering team, at the high-level ideas that were already being generated and, most of all, at the levels of enthusiasm and support from team members. They were already matching his excitement which he hadn't anticipated. They had already set up a number of key project teams with enthusiastic leaders. He had worked with the leaders to choose their teams. He had decided to give a light touch but wanted to be in touch enough so that he knew what was going on. He had developed a communication strategy for himself that would ensure that something was happening every day. He was fast becoming aware that he was the conductor of a large orchestra and

he needed to focus as much as anything on how he needed to change. Most of all he needed to focus on his own self-discipline. He had a big job to do in managing the firm and because this was important – (to him it was the most important and exciting thing; the one thing in his life that would create the greatest change and leave the greatest legacy) – he had to be disciplined in how he approached it. He realised that this was why he had taken on the job and now it was coming to fruition. He had briefed each of the leaders. He had even sent personal notes to their homes thanking them for taking on the task and reassuring them that he felt that they were exactly the right people, and that he would be there for them every step of the way. The project was under way which was exciting, but as he walked from his car and took the lift to his seventh-floor office he wondered just how he would maintain that enthusiasm and keep everyone on track and on purpose.

At this point we have learned a lot about the importance of creating a culture that is open to innovation and change and we have learned the importance of working together and teamwork. We have thought about how to create a competitive advantage to ensure our innovation is focused in the right way. We have learned about the need for strong, dynamic and enthusiastic leadership as well as the importance of good communication. We have set up a team to consider the many areas on which our innovation teams could focus and in the previous chapter we have looked at a number of areas that are ready for innovation across the industry.

But if we are to achieve our goals this chapter is key. And hard. No one likes conflict and we all prefer to give people the benefit of the doubt. Also, many of them are likely to be our friends. We will find it difficult to challenge them. But if the project is to succeed that is what we must do. We need to keep at the forefront of our minds that we are doing it for the benefit of the firm and for every partner and person in the firm. The firm will be a better and more successful place if we are successful. Our people will be happier each day. Our revenues and profits will be greater which will allow us to pay everyone more. People will feel proud of what they have achieved and proud that they were part of it. People will be proud of what others say about them and the firm.

But that just may not be enough. Process is key. Crucial to the success of any venture are people, process and product, and nowhere is process more important than when it comes to accountability. Greg Bustin, a well-respected US consultant, says that of all the data he has collected from more than 5,000 CEOs and their key executives around the world, lack of accountability is the single greatest threat to achieving consistent levels of high performance.[61]

In a survey of senior executives by the American Management Association, only 3% of executives described their companies as 'very successful' at executing their strategic plans (see www.amanet.org/training/articles/turning-strategy-into-execution.aspx).

It could be argued that innovation is not a project or a strategy but is a culture that encourages a free flow of thought. But we need to dispense with such thinking. Yes, culture is important but we are not inventing electricity. We are merely looking to find better ways of doing things and process is important to the delivery of results. A friend of mine who had recently got divorced in mid-life joined a number of dating sites. When I asked him why he had decided to do that, he told me that it was a numbers game and that he was aiming to have as many first dates as he could in order to find the right person. It did not seem very romantic but I could see his point. He had a process.

Successful businesses often have proven processes. These are likely to be the different stages of the delivery of service and may involve a number of touchpoints with the client. When you have worked out the proven process, it will be given a name.

Last year I went out to Kampala to work with a terrific charity, Retrak, now part of Hope for Justice who take the homeless children off the street, look after them and return them to their homes and parents. They have a proven process:

- they build good relationships with the local police force;
- the police will pick up children off the street usually as a result of a misdemeanour and take them to a Retrak home;
- they will wash and clothe them in a uniform, feed them and give them a bed;
- they will educate them and work with them to find out about their issues;
- they will locate their parents and visit them to try to resolve the issues and understand why they ran away; and
- when both parents and child are ready and are able to reconcile they will return them to their home.

That is a proven process. It is a process that delivers success almost every time. Process is really powerful in both designing success and delivering accountability. But there are ways of doing it.

It starts with the leader.

Ray Dalio in his terrific book *Principles*,[62] a must for any leader, writes "hold yourself accountable and appreciate them for holding you accountable".

It may feel uncomfortable at first but that will quickly disappear and people will value and respect you for your transparency. Do not just hide behind emails but hold meetings for everyone every three months or so, deliver a progress report and be prepared to ask questions. Ensure that all the project leaders are at the meeting. Think of it not just as you being accountable but as an opportunity to learn and refine your thoughts. Refer to it as the Listening Project, where you can take feedback from everyone. Ensure everyone in the room is relaxed and the meeting is fun and vibrant. If there are few questions, pick on one or two people who are positive and who you know will ask intelligent questions to get the meeting going. When you wrap up the meeting ensure that everyone knows that they can email you or call you separately with any further thoughts. Remember, people are always afraid of change so ensure that they feel part of it and are as comfortable with it as they can be. Do not be

"Do not just hide behind emails but hold meetings for everyone every three months or so, deliver a progress report and be prepared to ask questions."

a boss, be a colleague with the same ambitions and aims as they have. Be honest about your mistakes and vulnerabilities. You are looking for thoughtful discussion and the leader card is unhelpful. You need to be seen to be a doer who is helping them on a journey of which they are all a part. Thoughtful discussion and positive challenge is helpful to your cause. It tests you and shows you the things that are missing or that you have not thought of.

But you also need to hold each of your teams accountable. You are not trying to give orders here. People will only resent that and will look to defy them whenever they can. So before you introduce any processes you need to get them on your side. You need to kindle their passion and desire for the project but also the need to follow a process to deliver success. So you must get the balance right: enough process to deliver accountability without damaging the passion that you have begun. You do not want them dependent on you. You want them to be their own leaders but you want enough process to ensure success and some consistency. But holding people accountable means understanding them and their circumstances so that they have what they need to succeed. It is about understanding enough to set them up to succeed and not setting them up to fail. Always bear in mind that lots of people resent accountability. And even worse, they may not tell you that. You are the boss after all. So this is about using your emotional intelligence to set each leader up properly. However, the corollary to that is if you have done everything you can – listened to them, provided a light process and set them up to succeed – and they do not deliver what you need and are obviously not in sync with the other groups, then you have to act. Removing people who are not succeeding is the toughest job of any leader, in particular if they are a friend or you like the person. So you must remain objective and keep at the front of your mind that you are doing this for the firm and for the benefit of all the other employees in the business.

There may be different tools used by each team and you can create the bandwidth for each team to decide on its own tools. But it would be advisable for the project leader to complete at least one tool to present to you which will give you an idea of where each team is and demonstrates the process being made. I would encourage the use of vision/traction organisers described by Gino Wickman in his book *Traction*,[63] but of course there are others.

BHAG

Big hairy audacious goals (BHAG) was a concept first referred to by Jim Collins and Jerry Porras as mentioned earlier. This is not a budgeting process. No one will get shot for not hitting numbers. It is good to let the teams dream about what they are trying to achieve and it removes any shackles. It guards against focusing only on marginal improvement (though as you change the culture of the firm as a whole you will be looking for constant marginal improvements).

VTO

A vision/traction organiser (VTO) found in Gino Wickman's *Traction* is a very compact tool that could be used to manage projects. It is a two-page business plan. The first page has boxes where the team agrees its vision. You could include your BHAG. Another box will set out your values or courtesy rules as a group (how you will work together). One box could set out your passion (what is driving the group). Another box would show your proven process. Another section would set out where you aim to be in five years' time. Another box would show where you wish to be in three years' time and the measurables to achieve that, for example, the launch of new products or services, what the group looks like, how it is interacting with the firm, etc.

The first page is your vision and the second page is traction, that is, what needs to be done now. This again would be split into sections or boxes. The first box would have a 12-month target and would have space for measurables as well as a space for a list of things that you need to do during that time. The next box would show where you will be in three months, with space for a list of things that you need to do in that time.

"It is essential that all stakeholders are kept up to date with progress, whether that be the management committee or the board or the wider firm and so it is good to agree a strategy with the project leaders."

Wickman calls these 'rocks', referring to Stephen Covey's strategy of putting your rocks in place first, that is, the most important things that have to be done. Finally, the last box would be for the group to set out all the issues/challenges that they must address which, if they do not, will get in the way of success.

Not only does this tool dispel the notion that plans need to be 50 pages long but it gives greater focus as the team sets out to create a dynamic approach. Someone in the team needs to own the VTO and it must be adjusted every three months to take account of current activity and to ensure that everything is being addressed. Simplicity can be powerful.

I have already told the story of a chairman who had been sent a 100-page report from his HR director. When she came into his office he had two documents laid out on his desk face down. One was six pages long and one was her 100-page HR report. He asked her to point to the document that she thought was the most important. She immediately pointed to her own 100-page document. The chairman first of all turned over her 100-page document and then turned the six-page document over – the American Bill of Rights.

Communication programme

It is essential that all stakeholders are kept up to date with progress, whether that be the management committee or the board or the wider firm and so it is good to agree a strategy with the project leaders. One of the things in this may be your top five goals. These could be top five short-term goals and top five long-term goals. This is a great tool to keep you focused.

Communication has different sides to it but walking the four corners (W4C) is very important. Getting out and building relationships with not only the project leaders but all members of the teams shows how important you believe their role to be, and how glad you are that they are involved. Doing this every day or as often as you can is very important, as is taking the opportunity to tell stories that they will remember and take away.

You may have your own cardinals or cardinal rules that show how you think about leadership such as always treat people right, help people to set goals and take actions, communicate regularly and follow the policy of what gets measured, gets done (WGMGD). It will help them to relate to you.

One of the best ways of communicating is putting out a monthly leadership letter or blog. You have the advantage each month of repeating the goal and the importance of what they are doing as well as any successes. Obviously, you need to vary it, give some useful information that will help them but also use the opportunity to thank people for what they are doing and give any positive feedback.

You will from time to time have one-to-one direct reports with the project leaders. These are just short check-ins and will build trust and good communication. Make sure that you go armed with questions that will encourage your leader to talk about what they are doing but also reflect and learn from it. Have a plan for the meeting and ensure that your key questions have been answered. Summarise at the end what you have both learned. The meetings may start out weekly and may drop off to fortnightly, monthly or even less frequently once you are both comfortable and the communication lines have been established. You should be supporting, caring and helpful, but also focused: iron fist, velvet glove.

You may consider using professional coaches to work with each of your project leaders, particularly if you are aware that your reputation in the firm may mean that others would find it hard to open up to you. The coaches would be there to challenge the project leader but also to support and guide them in the project.

Ensure that from time to time you send personal thank-you notes to your project leaders, dropping them on their desks as you pass or, if you hot desk, sending them to their homes. Think every now and again how you can provide a small reward, the more personal the better, and make sure it has a handwritten note from you attached to it.

Creating transparency is key, as is creating a team ethos, so always talk in 'we' terms and never 'I' or 'you'. You want to build trust and you can help ensure that all team members feel equal through the careful use of language.

WGMGD

If you use the VTO process it will do a lot of the what gets measured, gets done (WGMGD) for you. What you are measuring at this stage is not financial metrics but behaviours and discipline. So you should sit down with your project leaders at least each quarter at your one-to-ones to go through his or her VTO and check on progress. Of course, if you have put financial investment into any project you will wish to check at this stage that you are within budget. Your job as coach is setting and agreeing the direction and then supporting, motivating and encouraging as much as you can. The VTO will be a very useful tool for you in doing both those things.

Focus on your five top goals, first in the short term to ensure they will be achieved and then in the long term to ensure that you are on track.

Rewards and saying "thank you"

One of the drivers throughout is to have fun. To publicly pat people on the back is a massive incentive for everyone, and it does not do any harm to inject a bit of competition. You can send the names of the winners of any competitions to everyone in the project teams and even to everyone in the firm. It is also important to show appreciation. Personal, handwritten "thank you" messages can be very powerful.

Team changes

Just like bringing on substitutes at a football match to change the game, it does not do any harm to add new blood to the team from time to time. It may be because you are reaching a critical point and you require, for example, new skills, a PR person or a systems manager. However, you should only do this by agreement with the project leader.

Executive PAs

Ensure that each team has an executive PA attached to them. Someone who will organise the meetings, the venues and ensure that everything is there, and who will send out reminders and action notes after the meetings confirming who is doing what and by when. That person should also ensure that the VTO is updated and that everyone has what they need at the beginning of each meeting. Being organised is very important. If the project leader is an organised person it is even more important that a good executive PA is part of the team. It takes a lot of the stress away, ensures that time is used efficiently and helps people to feel more professional.

Self-reflection letters

Some leaders find it a good exercise to write a letter to themselves at the end of the month setting out what happened during the month, what should have happened, and outlining what can be done differently next month. Again, it is a simple exercise to help you to focus. You are the person who can make it all happen. It takes only 30 minutes every month to write a letter to yourself and to keep that focus. Write it as if you are writing it to your board.

Quarterly get togethers/learning reviews

Every quarter bring your project leaders together and make the meeting fun. Start with good news but then ask open questions and encourage good debate. If they want to increase the momentum, encourage weekly or daily catch-ups. Stand up so everyone knows that these meetings are quick check-ins and not lengthy gatherings.

Celebrate successes

It is very important that you discuss and agree ways that you can celebrate when any of the teams have a success. Do not leave it to chance. Have a plan. Personal recognition and pats on the back create public recognition for the team and if one person has been instrumental in a success then blow his or her trumpet, create an awards system, and focus on winners. Be quick to acknowledge effort and success and others will follow your lead.

Accountability comes in lots of different ways. It is not just about key performance indicators (KPIs) which are far more suited to hard goals and targets. When dealing with behaviours and changes in culture you need to be far more sophisticated about your approach to accountability.

"Lawyers are very cautious animals who aim to get things 100% right before making the leap."

Chapter 9

Conclusion – a sense of urgency

The most successful entrepreneurs not only have courage and imagination, they also have a sense of urgency. They're not willing to wait. They have a burning desire to get something done.

Malcolm Gladwell

Failure can come in many forms but one of the real reasons will be the lack of urgency. This is particularly pertinent in law firms where lawyers are busy people and will always put their work (mistakenly) before anything else. You may have tried to create a 'burning platform' and demonstrated the consequences of what will happen if you do not act, but it is quite likely that you will not have convinced everyone fully of this. They will still be complacent. They may adjust their behaviour slightly as if they are in a house that requires some minor refurbishment but not the rebuild that you are looking for. This will play itself out in the pace at which their project groups move. Invite some partners to come in and talk to them, or possibly a consultant or two, and before you know it you have a talking shop with little or no delivery. When challenged they will have all sorts of wonderful excuses as to why they need to go at the pace they are. Lawyers are very cautious animals who aim to get things 100% right before making the leap. That does not work in this environment and if you wish to be successful you need to be fully cognisant of it and prepared for it.

Driving home the consequences of the 'burning platform' is clearly important. This needs to be done on an almost daily basis in the early stages. You need to be clever about it, showing what will happen if you do not get it right by demonstrating the consequences of failure to the business and showing the timeline that you feel you need to work to. Using your outside consultants to produce independent facts will help give more objectivity to this.

But far more important is winning the hearts of your people. I have no idea where the phrase 'to win the hearts and minds' comes from but I always find it significant that winning hearts comes first. All great movements have come about because great leaders have won the hearts of their followers. Martin Luther King Jr and Mahatma Gandhi are the perfect examples of that. In the case of King his impact on law, public discussion, culture and change is even more impressive when you consider he was a private citizen who never ran for public office and never held any official role within government. Yet, his impact and legacy was greater than almost any president. He was at his core a preacher and he would use his preaching to appeal to the hearts of his followers.

Gandhi first employed non-violent civil disobedience as an expatriate lawyer in South Africa, in the resident Indian community's struggle for civil rights. After his return to India in 1915, he set about organising peasants, farmers and urban labourers to protest against excessive land tax and discrimination.

In each case they won the hearts of their followers by their promotion of non-violent disobedience.

Successful change programmes are sustained by results. Finding small successes at an early stage is key. Holding such successes back until the launch of your innovation change programme may go some way to helping to sustain the programme, but until that point when the programme will generate its own momentum the way to create urgency is to win the hearts of both your project leaders and your people.

It is important that you behave with visible urgency every day. Your actions at this point once you have launched the programme are very important. Go out of your way to be visible and to show the need for urgency. Do not go for a coffee with your project leader without an aim, or without knowing what you need to get across, otherwise it is just going for a coffee. Make sure that your one-to-ones are properly planned so that your key points are conveyed. In all your communications at the early stage reach out to the hearts of your project leaders and all your people, and make it personal: "I do not want to be at the helm if this ship goes down, nor do you ..."; "We have a responsibility to everyone in this firm to create the best firm we can so they can have the best living they can ..."; "We owe this not just to us but to future generations ..."; "This firm has been around for 100 years and is important to this town, we all have a responsibility here ..."; "When I joined this firm I was proud and I want to be proud again. Do you?"

Guide your people so that they feel it in their hearts, not just their pockets. Create excitement so that it becomes a topic of conversation throughout the firm. Consider that you are creating a movement and feel the responsibility yourself of what you have begun. But it is not just a responsibility, it is a privilege to lead. You have been chosen to lead your firm; therefore, take on the mantle of making it great by leading change and innovation. Be the force multiplier of optimism. Show them what is possible, what can be achieved. Eleanor Roosevelt once said: "The future belongs to those who believe in the beauty of their dreams."[64] Drive forward confidently towards your dreams, harnessing the innovation and creativity around you to deliver all that you have dreamed of. But never forget that if you aspire to get to the very top, to reach first place, and you do not make it, it is no disgrace to stop at second or third place. As the All Blacks say, you will have left the shirt in a better place than you found it.

John's story

John left the office – it had been a long day. But very productive. He left the city with his favourite saxophonist, Joshua Redman, playing on Jazz FM. He had had a series of one-to-ones during the day and was surprised and delighted at some of the ideas that were being generated in the teams. He had encouraged them to think big but was amazed at just how big they were thinking. There were lots of ideas coming from the teams and some of them would be very easy to implement. It would be nice to see these early successes. He was already thinking about how they would communicate them, wanting the communications to come from the project leaders, and how they would celebrate. He could see now that the processes that they had put in place and the teamwork that they had worked so hard on was already paying dividends.

He let his mind drift to the mellow sax playing in his ear. He remembered that young idealistic John, wanting to be a lawyer and to change the world; proud of his profession, of the work he did and of his colleagues. Perhaps now he would be able to create that vision, not just for him but for the young Johns just starting out.

His phone rang. It was Vanessa. "Hi darling, what time will you be home? It has been so long since we sat and talked or even ate together. I've just booked Gino's for 8."

How good could life get?

Notes

1   John Kotter, *A Sense of Urgency* (Harvard Business Review Press, 2008).
2   David Kord Murray, *Borrowing Brilliance: The Six Steps to Business Innovation by Building on the Ideas of Others* (Random House Business, 2010).
3   Walter Isaacson, *The Innovators: How a Group of Inventors, Hackers, Geniuses and Geeks Created the Digital Revolution* (Simon & Shuster, 2015).
4   See Walter Isaacson, *The Innovators: How a Group of Inventors, Hackers, Geniuses and Geeks Created the Digital Revolution* (Simon & Shuster, 2015).
5   *Id.*
6   See https://deming.org/explore/fourteen-points.
7   See https://blog.toyota.co.uk/kaizen-toyota-production-system.
8   See Damian Hughes, *The Five Steps to a Winning Mindset: What Sport Can Teach Us About Great Leadership* (Macmillan, 2016).
9   See BBC News, Magazine, "Viewpoint: Should we all be looking for marginal gains?", www.bbc.co.uk/news/magazine-34247629.
10 Matthew Syed, *Black Box Thinking* (John Murray, 2016).
11 Daniel Kahneman, *Thinking, Fast and Slow* (Penguin, 2012).
12 Dan Ariely, *Predictably Irrational: The Hidden Forces That Shape Our Decisions* (Harper, 2009); Richard Thaler, *Nudge: Improving Decisions About Health,* *Wealth and Happiness* (Penguin, 2009).
13 See www.brainyquote.com/quotes/dale_carnegie_156636.
14 See https://seths.blog/2018/04/the-arrogance-of-listening-to-feedback/.
15 Malcolm Gladwell, *Blink: The Power of Thinking Without Thinking* (Penguin, 2006).
16 See www.goodreads.com/quotes/988332-some-people-say-give-the-customers-what-they-want-but.
17 Jim Collins and Jerry Porras, *Good to Great*, 1st edn (Random House Business, 2001); Jim Collins and Jerry Porras, *Built to Last: Successful Habits of Visionary Companies* (Random House Business, 2005).
18 See Jaynie Smith, *Creating Comprehensive Advantage* (Crown Business, 2006).
19 Jeremy Hope, Peter Bunce and Franz Röösli, *The Leader's Dilemma: How to Build an Empowered and Adaptive Organization Without Losing Control* (Wiley, 2011); Robert Bruce Shaw, *Extreme Teams: Why Pixar, Netflix, AirBnB, and Other Cutting-Edge Companies Succeed Where Most Fail* (AMACOM, 2017); Jim Collins and Jerry Porras, *Built to Last: Successful Habits of Visionary Companies* (Random House Business, 2005).
20 Paddi Lund, *Building the Happiness Centred Business*, 2nd edn (Solutions Press, 1995).

21 See James Kerr, *Legacy: What the All Blacks Can Teach Us About the Business of Life* (Constable, 2013).

22 Tom Peters, *Thriving on Chaos: Handbook for a Management Revolution* (HarperBusiness, 1989).

23 Damian Hughes, *The Barcelona Way: Unlocking the DNA of a Winning Culture* (Macmillan, 2018).

24 Robert Cialdini, *Influence: The Psychology of Persuasion* (HarperBusiness, 2007).

25 See Kevin Murray, *The Language of Leaders: How Top CEOs Communicate to Inspire, Influence and Achieve Results* (Kogan Page, 2011).

26 Jim Collins and Jerry Porras, *Built to Last: Successful Habits of Visionary Companies* (Random House Business, 2005).

27 Adam Grant, *Give and Take: Why Helping Others Drives Our Success* (W&N, 2014).

28 See Wikiquote, https://en.wikiquote.org/wiki/Warren_Buffett.

29 See Damian Hughes, *The Five Steps to a Winning Mindset: What Sport Can Teach Us About Great Leadership* (Macmillan, 2016).

30 James Surowiecki, *The Wisdom of Crowds: Why the Many Are Smarter Than the Few* (Abacus, 2005).

31 See www.brainyquote.com/quotes/mahatma_gandhi_105593.

32 Sir Ken Robinson, *Out of Our Minds* (Capstone, 2011).

33 James Clear, *Atomic Habits: An Easy and Proven Way to Build Good Habits and Break Bad Ones* (Random House Business, 2018).

34 See Wikiquote, https://en.wikiquote.org/wiki/Warren_Buffett.

35 Michael Porter, "The Comprehensive Advantage of Corporate Philanthropy", *Harvard Business Review*, 2002.

36 *Id.*

37 *Id.*

38 There are various versions of First they came.... See, eg, www.hmd.org.uk/resource/first-they-came-by-pastor-martin-niemoller/ and https://en.wikipedia.org/wiki/First_they_came_....

39 See www.brainyquote.com/quotes/joan_baez_132657.

40 See Simon Heffer, *High Minds: The Victorians and the Birth of Modern Britain* (Random House Books, 2013).

41 Tim Grover, *Relentless: From Good to Great to Unstoppable* (Scribner, 2014).

42 Hansard, 28 April 1909.

43 George Bernard Shaw, "Back to Methuselah", first performed 1922.

44 See Clayborne Carson (ed), *The Autobiography of Martin Luther King* (Abacus, 2000).

45 *Id.*

46 Chris Daffy, *Once a Customer, Always a Customer: How to Deliver Customer Service That Creates Customers for Life*, 3rd edn (Oak Tree Press, 2011).

47 Vernon Hill, *Fans not Customers* (Profile Books, 2012).

48 John Nordstrom at https://sharpencx.com/blog/nordstrom-customer-service/.

49 Patrick Lamb, Valorem Law Group in Mitchell Kowalski, *The Great Legal Reformation* (iUniverse, 2017).

50 See www.timpson-group.co.uk/about-timpson/upside-down-management/.

51 Peter Thiel, *Zero to One* (Virgin Books, 2015).

52 See Daniel Pink, *To Sell is Human: The Surprising Truth About Persuading, Convincing, and Influencing Others* (Canongate Books, 2018).

53 Lynda Gratton and Andrew Scott, *The 100-Year Life: Living and working in an age of Longevity* (Bloomsbury, 2016).

54 Steve Hilton, *More Human: Designing a World Where People Come First* (WH Allen, 2016).

55 Russell Sarder, *Building an Innovative Learning Organisation* (Wiley, 2016).

56 Daniel Pink, *To Sell is Human: The Surprising Truth About Persuading, Convincing, and Influencing Others* (Canongate Books, 2018).

57 Peter Thiel, *Zero to One* (Virgin Books, 2015).

58 See Daniel Priestley, *Oversubscribed: How to Get People Lining Up to Do Business with You* (Capstone, 2015).

59 Richard Susskind and Daniel Susskind, *The Future of the Professions: How Technology Will Transform the Work of Human Experts* (Oxford University Press, 2015).

60 www.telegraph.co.uk/technology/0/bill-gates-quotes-words-wisdom-microsoft-mogul/microsoft-corp-founder-bill-gates-gestures-launch-announcement/ .

61 Greg Bustin, *Accountability: The Key to Driving a High-Performance Culture* (McGraw-Hill Education, 2014).

62 Ray Dalio, *Principles: Life and Work* (Simon & Shuster, 2017).

63 Gino Wickman, *Traction: Get a Grip on Your Business* (BanBella Books, 2012).

64 See www.brainyquote.com/quotes/ eleanor_roosevelt_100940.

About the author

Darryl Cooke
Executive chairman, gunner*cooke* LLP
Darryl.Cooke@gunnercooke.com

Darryl Cooke began life as a barrister in Lincoln's Inn before joining the legal team of a major multinational corporation. He started working in private practice at SJ Berwin, where he quickly grew a thriving private equity practice, and he continued at Addleshaws, where he started what soon became one of the firm's strongest practice areas, joining the board at the same time. He later moved to DLA Piper where he headed private equity in EMEA.

In 2010 Darryl set up the game-changing law firm, gunner*cooke*, with its unique model to challenge the leading law firms. gunner*cooke* is now one of the fastest growing law firms in the UK.

Darryl has always had entrepreneurial instincts: alongside existing work commitments he established a property company and a business conference company, and he also realised his dream of owning a pub. He has also served as a director of numerous businesses in various industries and has established inspire*, gunnercooke's charitable foundation.

Having worked across all parts of the legal industry as well as in other sectors, Darryl is well equipped to consider the legal profession and its need for innovation. He is passionate about the legal industry, which he describes as his first love, and he is equally passionate that it must change in order to continue to be effective.

Darryl is also author of Sweet & Maxwell's *Private Equity: Law and Practice*, now in its sixth edition and sold in 40 countries.

Bibliography

Some of the books below are directly referred to in this book while others have just influenced my thinking.

Bustin, Greg, *Accountability: The Key to Driving a High-Performance Culture* (McGraw-Hill Education, 2014)

Carson, Clayborne (ed), *The Autobiography of Martin Luther King* (Abacus, 2000)

Chapman, Bob and Raj Sisodia, *Everybody Matters: The Extraordinary Power of Caring for Your People Like Family* (Penguin, 2015)

Christensen, Clayton, *Competing Against Luck: The Story of Innovation and Customer Choice* (HarperBusiness, 2016)

Cialdini, Robert, *Influence: The Psychology of Persuasion* (HarperBusiness, 2007)

Clear, Jim, *Atomic Habits: An Easy and Proven Way to Build Good Habits and Break Bad Ones* (Random House Business, 2018)

Collins, Jim and Jerry Porras, *Built to Last: Successful Habits of Visionary Companies* (Random House Business, 2005)

Collins, James and Jerry Porras, *Good to Great*, 1st edn (Random House Business, 2001)

Clegg, Brian, *Capturing Customers' Hearts* (FT/Prentice Hall, 2000)

Csikszentmihalyi, Mihaly, *Creativity: The Psychology of Discovery and*

Invention (Harper Perennial, 2013)

Daffy, Chris, *Once a Customer Always a Customer: How to Deliver Customer Service That Creates Customers for Life*, 3rd edn (Oak Tree Press, 2011)

Dalio, Ray, *Principles: Life and Work* (Simon & Shuster, 2017)

Friedman, Stewart, *Total Leadership: Be a Better Leader, Have a Richer Life* (Harvard Business Review Press, 2008)

Gladwell, Malcolm, *Blink: The Power of Thinking Without Thinking* (Penguin, 2006)

Grant, Adam, *Give and Take: Why Helping Others Drives Our Success* (W&N, 2014)

Gratton, Lynda and Andrew Scott, *The 100-Year Life: Living and working in an age of Longevity* (Bloomsbury, 2016)

Grover, Tim, *Relentless: From Good to Great to Unstoppable* (Scribner, 2014)

Hayman, Michael and Nick Giles, *Mission: How the Best in Business Break Through* (Portfolio Penguin, 2016)

Heffer, Simon, *High Minds: The Victorians and the Birth of Modern Britain* (Random House Books, 2013)

Hill, Vernon, *Fans not Customers* (Profile Books, 2012)

Hilton, Steve, *More Human: Designing a World Where People Come First* (WH Allen, 2016)

Holden, Reed and Mark Burton, *Pricing with Confidence: 10 Ways to Stop Leaving Money on the Table* (Wiley, 2008)

Hope, Jeremy, Peter Bunce and Franz Röösli, *The Leader's Dilemma: How to Build an Empowered and Adaptive Organization Without Losing Control* (Wiley, 2011)

Hughes, Damian, *The Barcelona Way: Unlocking the DNA of a Winning Culture* (Macmillan 2018)

Hughes, Damian, *The Five Steps to a Winning Mindset: What Sport Can Teach Us About Great Leadership* (Macmillan, 2016)

Isaacson, Walter, *The Innovators: How a Group of Inventors, Hackers, Geniuses and Geeks Created the Digital Revolution* (Simon & Shuster, 2015)

Kahneman, Daniel, *Thinking, Fast and Slow* (Penguin, 2012)

Kelley, Thomas, *The Art of Innovation* (Profile Books, 2002)

Kerr, James, *Legacy: What the All Blacks Can Teach As About the Business of Life* (Constable, 2013)

Kotter, John, *A Sense of Urgency* (Harvard Business Review Press, 2008)

Kowalski, Mitchell, *The Great Legal Reformation* (iUniverse, 2017)

Kramers, Kraig, *CEO Tools: The Nuts-n-Bolts of Business for Every Manager's Success* (Gandy Dancer Press, 2002)

Lerner, Josh, *The Architecture of innovation: The Economics of Creative Organizations* (Harper Business Review Press, 2012)

Lund, Paddi, *Building the Happiness Centred Business*, 2nd edn (Solutions Press, 1995)

Macdivitt, Harry and Mike Wilkinson, *Value-Based Pricing: Drive Sales and Boost Your Bottom Line by Creating, Communicating and Capturing Customer Value* (McGraw-Hill Professional, 2011)

McCord, Patty, *Powerful: Building a Culture of Freedom and Responsibility* (Missionday, 2018)

Metaxas, Eric, *Bonhoeffer: Pastor, Martyr, Prophet, Spy* (Thomas Nelson, 2011)

Murray, David Kord, *Borrowing Brilliance: The Six Steps to Business Innovation by Building on the Ideas of Others* (Random House Business, 2010)

Murray, Kevin, *The Language of Leaders: How Top CEOs Communicate to Inspire, Influence and Achieve Results* (Kogan Page, 2011)

Nonaka, Ikujiro and Horotaka Takeuchi, *The Knowledge Creating Company: How Japanese Companies Create the Dynamics of Innovation* (OUP, 1995)

Partridge, Dale, *People over Profit* (HarperCollins, 2015)

Peters, Tom, *Thriving on Chaos: Handbook for a Management Revolution* (HarperBusiness, 1989)

Pink, Daniel, *To Sell is Human: The Surprising Truth About Persuading, Convincing, and Influencing Others* (Canongate Books, 2018)

Porter, Michael, "The Comprehensive Advantage of Corporate

Philanthropy", *Harvard Business Review*, 2002

Priestly, Daniel, *Oversubscribed: How to Get People Lining Up to Do Business with You* (Capstone, 2015)

Robinson, Sir Ken, *Out of Our Minds* (Capstone, 2011)

Rushkoff, Douglas, *Get Back in the Box: How Being Great at What You Do Is Great for Business* (HarperBusiness, 2007)

Sarder, Russell, *Building an Innovative Learning Organisation* (Wiley, 2016)

Service, Owain and Rory Gallagher, *Think Small: The Surprisingly Simple Ways to Reach Big Goals* (Michael O'Mara, 2017)

Shaw, Robert Bruce, *Extreme Teams: Why Pixar, Netflix, AirBnB, and Other Cutting-Edge Companies Succeed Where Most Fail* (AMACOM, 2017)

Smith, Jaynie, *Creating Competitive Advantage: Give Customers a Reason to Choose You Over Your Competitors* (Crown Business, 2006)

Spector, Robert and Breanne Reeves, *The Nordstrom Way to Customer Experience Excellence: Creating a Values-Driven Service Culture* (Wiley, 2017)

Susskind, Richard and Daniel, *The Future of the Professions: How Technology Will Transform the Work of Human Experts* (OUP, 2015)

Syed, Matthew, *Black Box Thinking* (John Murray, 2016)

Thiel, Peter, *Zero to One* (Virgin Books, 2015)

Watkinson, Matt, *The Ten Principles Behind Great Customer Experiences* (FT Press, 2012)

Weiss, Alan, *Value-Based Fees: How to Charge – and Get – What You're Worth*, 2nd edn (Wiley, 2008)

Weylman, Richard, *The Power of Why: Breaking Out In a Competitive Marketplace* (Amazon Publishing, 2013)

Wickman, Gino, *Traction: Get a Grip on Your Business* (BanBella Books, 2012)

Zenger, Tod, *Building Competitive Advantage: How to Solve the Puzzle of Sustaining Growth While Creating Value* (HarvardBusiness Review Press, 2016)

Index

About Globe Law and Business

Globe Law and Business was established in 2005, and from the beginning, we set out to create law books which are sufficiently high level to be of real use to the experienced professional, yet still accessible and easy to navigate. Most of our authors are drawn from Magic Circle and other top commercial firms, both in the UK and internationally.

Our titles are carefully produced, with the utmost attention paid to editorial, design and production processes. We hope this results in high-quality books which are easy to read, and a pleasure to own. All our new books are also available as ebooks, which are compatible with most desktop, laptop and tablet devices.

We have recently expanded our portfolio to include a new range of journals, Special Reports and Good Practice Guides, available both digitally and in hard copy format, and produced to the same high standards as our books.

We'd very much like to hear from you with your thoughts and ideas for improving what we offer. Please do feel free to email me on sian@globelawandbusiness.com with your views.

Sian O'Neill, Managing director
Globe Law and Business